FROM THE
LIBRARY OF

Soby's

Soby's

NEW SOUTH CUISINE

By Rodney Freidank, Carl Sobocinski, David Williams

with Richard Peck

Photographs by Stephen Stinson

Table 301™

Greenville, South Carolina

Published by
Table 301™
207 South Main Street
Greenville, SC 29601
(864) 232-7007

Book Design: Nancy Cutler, Midnight Oil Design, LLC
Editor: Susan B. Peck
Digital Producer: Wayne Culpepper, FishEye Studios
Project Intern: Abby Culin

Visit us on the Web *www.sobys.com.*

ISBN: 978-0-9797945-0-6

Printed in the United States of America

10 9 8 7 6 5 4 3 2 1

We dedicate this book to the guests and staff of Table 301,
without whom Soby's would not exist.

ᴏᴏᴏᴏᴏ

And to Mike Goot

Rodney: "You are a die-hard 'foodie' and have lived vicariously through us for the past ten years. You remind
us constantly that the Soby's experience should excite all the senses, not just the taste buds."

David: "Your out-of-the-box thinking has kept us on our toes and encouraged us to become
more than we ever thought we could be. You are a great friend and mentor."

Carl: "Your passion and commitment to excellence is infectious. The Soby's brand wouldn't be
what it is today without your extra effort and dedication.
We love you and cherish your friendship. Thank you for all you do for us."

ᴏᴏᴏᴏᴏ

TABLE OF CONTENTS

ooooo

TABLE OF CONTENTS

ooooo

TABLE OF CONTENTS

ooooo

TABLE OF CONTENTS

ooooo

FOREWORD

I met Carl Sobocinski back in the early '90s when he had an amazing restaurant called The 858 in Greenville. I had just moved from Charleston to New York after culinary school. I would hit The 858 a few times a year, when I had the chance to visit my folks who live in Greenville.

The 858 was the first time since Vince Perone's that a restaurateur brought a real concept to Greenville—and this one was downtown! Carl enlisted a chef from the Buckhead Diner in Atlanta and The 858 was the talk of the town. Dinner there was loud, delicious, and high energy. Carl had a vision for both the restaurant and for Greenville. He brought fresh ideas, woke up the semi-sleepy Main Street, and created a reason to get dressed and meet your friends for dinner. He made Greenville feel like a city that was on the verge of being something big. Lucky for all of us, The 858 didn't work out. It was just a test run for what Carl really had up his sleeve.

Soby's opened in 1997 and Greenville never looked back. It was the Upstate's finest restaurant. Big City meets Deep South. Fast forward ten crazy years to 2007, and Chefs David Williams and Rodney Freidank have never been more on top of their game. The food is amazing, bold, and steeped deep in the tradition of great Southern cooking. Soby's is like having the flavors of the Lowcountry, Atlanta, and New Orleans all delivered through the gifted hands of these incredibly talented chefs. It is the

Southern food I love taken to a whole different level. I can't walk out of Soby's without having the smoked Port Royal shrimp with sweet corn cakes and the apple butter spiked with jalapeños, or the baked oysters with andouille and crawfish tail stuffing. I've asked David and Rodney for the recipes for everything from their crab cakes to the incredible pimiento cheese hush puppies on their hickory planked salmon. Apparently, so have a lot of other people. That's why this book is such a good idea.

Turning through the pages of *Soby's New South Cuisine* is like reading a map of where the flavors of modern Southern cuisine are going. It's bold, it's hip, and it's as delicious as regional American cooking gets. I have a few hundred cookbooks in my library at home, but there is a special slot for this one. Not just because Soby's is a great restaurant or the recipes in this book are the way I like to cook at home. It's because Carl Sobocinski has made my hometown a great place to call home. To Carl, congratulations on ten amazing years in Greenville. To David and Rodney, keep on cooking guys—you make my mouth water. And to you the reader who is thinking about dinner tonight, *Soby's New South Cuisine* really delivers.

Tyler Florence

San Francisco, California

2007

Carl Sobocinski

"David and I talked about all kinds of concepts. I had written a business plan calling the restaurant 'The Newsroom.' Tickers across the bottom of TV screens were new. CNN was still a fresh concept. *The Greenville News* was nearby. We would have old newspapers framed and hung on the walls. The menu would be printed daily.

"Then I saw 207 South Main Street, and I knew it was the spot."

"Exactly. One look at the location and I knew Carl was right. The building had incredible potential. Packed with personality, it spoke to us and said 'conceptually you're off the mark.' At about thirty feet wide and over one hundred feet deep, some saw a bowling alley. We didn't. It reminded us of the Southern townhomes we had seen from my native Alexandria, Virginia, to Savannah, Georgia, and on to New Orleans, Louisiana.

"New South Cuisine seemed a natural fit, and since Carl had already established a reputation for hospitality in Greenville, we would call it Soby's."

David Williams

Carl: "Although I had some success at The 858 in Greenville, while David was in Hilton Head, neither of us could have guessed at the success Soby's would achieve. We certainly didn't envision the path we would take, either—from our first *Fall for Greenville*, when we prepared our dishes in the Greenville Country Club's kitchen, to our down-to-the-wire Grand Opening in November 1997 without the front doors on the restaurant. And who could have imagined the hundreds of wonderful friends we would make, and loyal guests we would serve, since Soby's opened?"

David: "We knew we could make people comfortable, make them feel welcome, and prepare great food. But we'd been working like madmen every day for months to get the building ready. Like so many old buildings, the natural beauty had been masked by cheap paneling, dropped ceilings, and glued-down indoor/ outdoor carpeting, which took forever to get up. We did all the rough carpentry. I'm a chef—and although Carl has a degree in architecture, neither of us had ever built anything on this scale. We learned construction techniques from friends who helped when they could, and it became a real family effort. My son, Austin, even learned to walk in our hard-hat zone!"

YOU'RE OPENING A RESTAURANT WHERE?

Soby's location has always been at the center of Greenville's history. Greenville was actually founded on Soby's doorstep, exactly 200 years before the restaurant opened. In 1797, settler Lemuel James Alston drew up plans for what he called "Greenville Court House Village of Pleasantburg," quickly shortened to Greenville. Alston built a two-story mansion called Prospect Hill for himself, and offered 52 lots for sale spread over eight blocks—all of them surrounding what is today's Court Square. A courthouse was drawn in the middle of Alston's plan for Greenville, at a location that corresponds to today's Court Street—just outside Soby's front doors.

Fast-forward about 150 years. Commercial development moved northward along Main Street, but for all intents and purposes downtown was dying, having fallen victim to the shopping malls that began appearing in the 1960s. Beautiful old storefronts were covered with "modern" plastic and steel facades. Other architectural gems, like City Hall and the Ottaray Hotel, were demolished. Reedy River Falls was covered with a four-lane concrete overpass. And once the sun set? It was a ghost town. You could almost hear old Lemuel turning over in his grave.

The Soby's Story Timeline of Events

November 7, 1997
Opening night at Soby's

April 18, 1998
Mark Andrews rings in Table 21 at 5:55 pm for our $1 Millionth sale

August 1998
First *Wine Spectator* Award of Excellence

Enter Charles Daniel, Buck Mickel, Roger C. Peace, Max Heller, and a handful of other entrepreneurial visionaries who refused to let downtown Greenville die. Charles Daniel began this trend, erecting Daniel Construction's corporate headquarters at the north end of Main Street. Roger Peace, of Peace Multimedia did the same, building a new facility for *The Greenville News* (now owned by Gannett) at the south end of Main Street. Soon after, through an innovative public/private partnership, construction of the Hyatt Regency in 1982 established an additional anchor at the north end of Main Street. This step provided the first hints about what downtown 21st century Greenville might become: a real destination, offering a variety of dining and shopping experiences—a place people would come, even would live, after dark.

TIMING IS EVERYTHING

Carl: "In 1993, I came to the *Downtown Alive* festival and was impressed by the energy and vitality I saw there. A friend had just purchased the old Elks Lodge #858 on East North Street. He and I saw potential for a restaurant on the second floor, where the kitchen and dining room had been. We put together a plan. The 858 is also where Chef Rodney Freidank and I met, and we've worked together almost continuously since that time. Several other staff members of the Soby's opening crew started at The 858: David Dunning, whom we nicknamed "Soup;" David Anctil known as the "Face" to hundreds of guests across the Upstate; Richard O'Reilly, Von Washington, Frank Kapp, and Pam Jordan, the original pastry chef at Soby's.

"When I left The 858 in January 1996, I took a couple of months off and then, at the ripe old age of 29, started putting together a business plan for another restaurant. I also started scouting out possible downtown locations—including the old Gargoyle Club, where Sassafras is located today, and Connolly's, then a shag club three or four nights of the week."

David: "Carl and I weren't new to the Upstate when we decided to launch Soby's. We had worked together at Keowee Key Country Club, while Carl was in school at Clemson University. My wife, Mary, and I were in Hilton Head when Carl called about The 858. It wasn't the right time. I had just established myself on the coast; it was an absolutely wonderful place to live and work. If it hadn't been for the hurricane season of 1996, we might never have left.

September 3, 1998

Bi-Lo Center opens with Janet Jackson Concert

November 1998

Elton John at Bi-Lo Center – David, Frank, and Carl drive several guests to concert because their dinner ran too long and they needed to rush

February 14, 1999

Guest Chefs Chef Paul Prudhomme and Chef Keith Keogh dinner at Soby's for Pendleton Place, arranged by friend and mentor, Jim Cockman

BEFORE: 1997

Above: *Cancellation Shoe Mart after purchase but before the transformation to Soby's begins*
At left: *David Williams, Austin Williams (age, 6 months), Carl Sobocinski*

Images from the Soby's Archives

January 2000

Soby's and Augusta Grill serve dinner at the James Beard House during a blizzard

June 22, 2000

Carl and David sign lease on space at Poinsett Plaza for future restaurant, a project that would take about three years to complete

October 22, 2000

Historic Poinsett Hotel reopens its doors as Westin Poinsett after thirteen years of vacancy

AFTER: 2007

Above: Soby's completely renovated and serving guests for ten years

At right: David Williams, Austin Williams (age, 10 years), Carl Sobocinski

March 28, 2001

Soby's on the Side deli and bakery opens

April 26-29, 2001

First BMW Charity Pro-Am at the Cliffs (tournament was the BUY.Com Pro-Am then); celebrities included Kevin Costner and Rudy Gatlin

July 1-8, 2001

Carl's first wine education trip to Napa with staff

"But after two evacuations, during which we drove to Greenville to stay with Carl, it became clear to me that running a restaurant in Hilton Head was a risky proposition. With a season that is only about fifteen weeks long, between Memorial Day and Labor Day, those weeks are essential for restaurants to hit their financial goals. I started looking for a place that was a better bet. Mary and I were expecting Austin, our first son, and Greenville looked like a great place to raise kids. So, when Carl called, and we started talking about the possibility of opening a restaurant together in downtown Greenville, it didn't take long to decide."

Carl: "Most successful enterprises are as much the result of good timing as of vision and hard work. The stars were aligning: as David was considering coming back to the Upstate and I was searching for a restaurant site, the owner of the Cancellation Shoe Mart, Carl Proser, decided he was ready to retire. The Peace Center for the Performing Arts on South Main Street, just one-half block from Cancellation Shoe Mart, had been completed in 1990. That paved the way for the re-emergence of South Main as the hub of downtown. In late fall of 1996, we came to terms on the Shoe Mart building. The sale closed in January 1997.

"Once the building was purchased, good friend Frank Kapp joined me to begin plans for

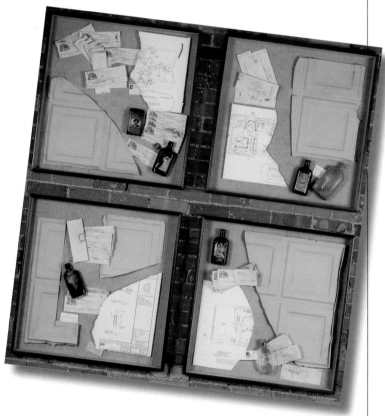

Above: Artifacts from restoration of The Loft, now displayed in a shadowbox in The Loft dining room
Opposite: Reedy River flows under South Main Street

demolition. We shared the news with David, who finalized his move to Greenville soon after. Frank was instrumental in so much of what we did during that year and the years following. He basically took the year off and threw himself into the construction project. He tackled everything he did with the same passion and ability. Once the restaurant opened with David as Chef, and me running the front-of-the-house, Frank took control of the wine program and put Soby's on the map. We won *Wine Spectator* magazine's 'Award of Excellence' before we'd even been open for a year."

July 27, 2001
First event in The Loft, for Brian O'Rourke's going away reception

August 13, 2001
Far Niente wine dinner, with Ashley Heisey

September 11, 2001
Soby's grieves with the rest of America; slowest night in the history of Soby's

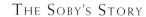

Images from the Soby's Archives

Top left: *Cancellation Shoe Mart, looking toward what is Soby's kitchen today* **Top right:** *Cancellation Shoe Mart looking toward Main Street, Soby's dining room and bar today* **Middle left:** *Removing layers of wall materials to reveal Soby's brick walls* **Middle right:** *Removing Cancellation Shoe Mart acoustical tile ceiling to expose the skylight* **Bottom left:** *The first bricked-in window is reopened, looking toward what is Devereaux's restaurant today* **Bottom right:** *Replacing plate glass windows with Soby's front doors to Main Street*

October 15, 2001

Schug wine dinner sets record event attendance with 200 guests for a five-course dinner with wines, hosted by Axel and Christine Schug

May 2002

Chef Michael Granata becomes partner in Soby's on the Side and creates Soby's Catering, taking Soby's hospitality to a new dimension

November 10, 2002

Soby's Five Year Anniversary Party

CREATING SOBY'S ON A SHOESTRING

David: "Once the building was purchased and work started inside, all kinds of people would stop by to talk. Some would say, 'Oh, you'll never make it—why on earth did you buy in this part of town?' Others stopped by looking for jobs. Family and friends supported our efforts all the way, with many of them actually helping with demolition and construction—restoring the beauty of this old building.

"The building was a grocery in the 1880s. Then it served as County Dispensary #1, a state-owned liquor store, in the early 1890s. I guess making it into a place people come for food and drink a hundred years later kind of returned it to its roots.

"Best we can tell from the local historians, the building operated as a cotton warehouse in the late 1890s, serving the textile mills along the Reedy River. The skylight was put in at that time to bring in natural light to grade the cotton. There's also a concrete pad where a large scale sat. There was so much concrete in the pad and the supporting pillars in the basement, we couldn't remove it. Instead, we turned it into a 'feature' by painting the Soby's logo on it."

Carl: "The building's longest running tenant was Jones Furniture Store from 1930 until almost 1968. Along with bottles we found in the walls and ceilings from the Dispensary, we discovered several old ledgers and checks from the furniture store. Those are all displayed in The Loft today.

"We learned so much about the building by doing restoration. The original building ended about where the downstairs fireplace is. You can actually see the former floor level, marked by a ledge along the walls three feet higher than the current floor. We discovered the fireplace after ripping off the wallboard that was covering it. Everything beyond the fireplace, extending out toward Main Street, was probably constructed in 1937, based on a date scratched on an I-beam above the doors looking out on Main."

David: "You know, I think all we went through together made a real difference in Soby's hospitality. Take the fireplace, for instance. The new stone face and hearth was built by staff—staff who had never done stonework. We all just did what we had to do. And that brought the team together. It made Soby's their place, too. That's what carried over into the way we treated guests, and still does. We built this place together, with our bare hands, for our guests. Soby's is no faceless, nameless corporation. This is our home away from home and we've tried to make it that for our guests, as well."

November 18, 2002

Master of Wine Michael Broadbent hosts tasting and book signing in The Loft

January 1, 2003

Carl and David form Court Square Restaurant Group, parent company for Soby's, Soby's on the Side, and Restaurant O

January 14 – 15, 2003

Carl and Danny Baker pass Court of Master Sommelier Level I exam

Top left:
Construction
forming the shape
of Soby's bar
Top right: *Soby's*
bar takes shape
Middle left: *Frank*
Kapp, David, and
David's son, Austin,
stand on newly installed kitchen hood
The only access? Jump from the mezzanine at left ***Middle right:***
Booths were installed with beadboard sides milled by Chef
David from unneeded ceiling beams ***Bottom left:*** *Renovating*
the Main Street store front brick by brick ***Bottom right:*** *Chef*
Rodney and Soby's original pastry chef, Pam Jordan, tile
bathroom walls

Images from the Soby's Archives

February 10 – 16, 2003

Chef Rodney spends Valentine's week working at Charlie Trotter's restaurant in Chicago, learns what cold really means

April 12, 2003

First Saturday Farmer's Market event on Court Street (Carl was co-chairman for the Market)

May 1, 2003

BMW Celebrity Party and Grand Opening of Restaurant O. with celebrity guests including Cheech Marin, Kevin Costner, John O'Hurley, and Gabrielle Reece

CREATING
NEW SOUTH CUISINE

Rodney: "When Carl and David decided that the restaurant would serve 'New South Cuisine,' it was the building itself that spoke to them. Seeing the hand-hewn beams and handmade bricks, they gained a real sense of the history of Greenville and the comfortable feeling that always comes from familiar places, familiar people, and familiar ingredients.

"As they transformed the old building by milling the wood from the ceilings into beadboard for the booths (a task David did himself) and accentuated the building's natural warmth with bright modern accents, like the painted ceilings and pendant lamps, I think it occurred to them that the same could be done with food. That's where I came into the picture.

"Together, we set out to create a cuisine that reflected both the heritage and the dynamic energy of our community. In essence, we wanted to give a facelift to Southern cooking, using indigenous ingredients and traditional

Chef Rodney Freidank

preparations but presented with a fresh new look and bold new flavors—hence the term 'New South Cuisine.'

"First, the 'South.' We committed ourselves to using fresh ingredients, as Greenvillians had for generations, by building relationships with local farmers and producers of fine artisanal products. We chose authentic ingredients and flavors from all parts of the Southeast—Virginia to Louisiana—to serve as our culinary foundation.

"Next, the 'New.' We wanted to create dishes that would reflect Greenville's changing population and increasing stature as an international business hub by incorporating Asian, Latino, and Mediterranean ingredients and cooking techniques. We weren't so much aiming to create cutting-edge cuisine, but to provide our guests with satisfying, comforting food that surprises and delights.

"And equally important to us was the wine experience at Soby's. We believe that wine is food. The ability for wine to make food taste better, and for food to make wine taste better, was something we wanted to develop and share with our guests—and we did!"

June 12-15, 2003

Carl attends Aspen Food and Wine Festival. Southern Exposure idea is conceived

October 20, 2003

NYC Chef's Guild awards Carl and David the Italo C. Granata Lifetime Achievement Award

November 14, 2003

Elliott Davis leads Greenville's "Fastest Growing Companies." Court Square Restaurant Group nominated

OPENING NIGHT DRAWS NEAR

As Carl and David saw the restaurant taking shape, they set the date for opening night. Teaser invitations were sent out for guests to come experience Soby's on Friday, November 7, 1997. As autumn days grew shorter and nights became longer, the team worked well into the dark.

Above: Opening Night invitation

Rodney: "Four days before opening, restaurant inspectors visited our site. David, Carl, and I will never forget that visit. There was a toolbox in the middle of the floor; the kitchen equipment wasn't fully installed. The inspector told us, 'I've been doing this for twenty-five years. I've seen a lot of restaurants open and I've heard a lot of people say they'll be finished on time. From what I'm seeing here, you aren't going to make it.'

"Carl and David gathered the team and said, 'Decide now, if we're going to do it.' Tired as we were, we decided. Unanimously. We worked around the clock—assembling tables, putting in the booths, squaring away the kitchen. When the inspector came back for final inspection, he said, 'I can't believe it. I've never seen a team do anything like this.'"

A NIGHT TO REMEMBER

The inspections were finished. Equipment was in place. Final opening night invitations included details, along with an empty compact disc case to be filled with that guest's favorite music and brought as the price of admission. More than 200 CDs were brought that night! Right from the beginning our guests would be comfortable, listening to the same music they enjoyed at home.

Carl: "What can any of us say about opening night? We were opening a restaurant with the largest dining room downtown. Despite our hope that Soby's would be well received, we were on pins and needles. Maybe the only thing that helped with some of those opening night jitters

January 20, 2004

Carl nominated as Greenville "Business Person of the Year" (one of five)

September 10, 2004

Liberty Bridge, an award winning, world class attraction designed to maximize the beauty of its surroundings, opens at Falls Park

January 14, 2005

Carl and David take staff who have been with Soby's for seven years to Las Vegas

Patio photograph by Mark Andrews

January 18, 2005

Greenville restaurants cook
lunch for Southern Living
writers in Birmingham, AL

February 3, 2005

Court Square Restaurant Group signs
agreement to take space in the Hampton
Inn and Suites building at River Place

August 26, 2005

Stephen Corley, Monticello
winemaker dinner

was the morning paper, November 7, 1997. *The Greenville News* announced that Westin Hotels would be restoring the Poinsett Hotel across the street from us. Court Square truly was becoming the heart of Greenville once again.

"Opening night itself? It was not only the culmination of our team's hard work, but also the beginning of a dream that still hasn't ended. So many friends today were here that night. A lot of them even helped with construction. It wasn't just an opening—it was a celebration! The celebration is still going on; dozens of the very same guests dine with us today. We have completed our first ten years, but as they say, 'You ain't seen nothin' yet!'

"Mike Goot, who was instrumental in helping work out the Soby's concept and marketing from before the time we opened, once said, 'Given the large and very well-known failure rate of restaurants, restaurant years must be something akin to dog years.' And yes, our tenth anniversary is an accomplishment we are humbled by, but also very proud of. Mike sent a note of encouragement when he heard about the cookbook. I can't think of a better way to close the first ten years of the Soby's story, and to enter the next ten, than to include Mike's note.

Above: *Original management team, from left to right, Frank Kapp, Lisa Griffin, Rodney Freidank, David Williams, Pam Jordan, Carl Sobocinski*

Ten years counts for a lot! In Soby's, you crafted something solid and enduring, which is much harder than jumping on the culinary trend du jour and riding the short, steep trajectory of flash-in-the-pan success. You have truly found a recipe for success.

"We offer you—our guests and friends—some of those recipes now."

Rodney: "Wait a cotton-picking minute! Opening night wasn't quite as celebratory as all that—at least not at first. Sure the hood was shiny and new and the fireplace was lit for the very first time. Servers' uniforms were pressed and starched. Not a chip could be found on any of the plates. The kitchen was a blur of activity

Image from the Soby's Archives

September 11, 2005

CSRG organizes and participates with many local restaurants in New Orleans Brunch on Main St. raising $40k for Hurricane Katrina relief efforts

September 15, 2005

Economic Development Group from Fort Wayne, IN, comes to study Greenville's growth and downtown development. Court Square Restaurant Group hosts receptions and dinners. Carl speaks to group as part of a panel

January 15-27, 2006

Soby's kitchen undergoes massive remodeling, turning it into a state-of-the-art show kitchen

Top left: *Mary and David Williams* **Top right:** *Chef David Williams with parents Betty and Kirk* **Bottom left:** *Carl Sobocinski and Soby's marketing strategist, Mike Goot* **Bottom right:** *Carl Sobocinski with parents Bob and Anne*

Images from the Soby's Archives

January 20-21, 2006

Red Cross Fine Wine Auction raises $255K. Wine Celebrities include Brian and Claudia Fleury, Fleury Vineyards; Larry McGuire, Nickel and Nickel; and Philippe Thibault, Chateau St. Jean, among others

April 24, 2006

Court Square restaurants go smoke-free voluntarily

April 26, 2006

Gary Player announces plans for partnership and relocation of his corporate headquarters to The Cliff's at Mountain Park, including design of a Gary Player Signature Golf Course

and aromas. Everything was as it should be. What could possibly go wrong?

"Then it happened. One question from a server brought the kitchen to a screeching halt. 'Chef, what do you want us to serve butter for the bread on?'

"Bread? Bread wasn't on the construction punch list. Bread wasn't on any of the order guides used to purchase ingredients. Bread wasn't on the 200 menus we had proofread and printed. Bread? There was none anywhere in the restaurant. We had forgotten that, with anticipated waits of up to two hours for a seat (we didn't take reservations when we opened), our guests might like to have some bread when they sat down.

"Chef David roared into action. 'Slice the butter and place it on the bread and butter plates,' was his answer to the server. And with that he headed back into the kitchen and grabbed a bowl. A little flour, a little shortening, a little of this and a little of that—and there they were— just like we had planned them all along: Soby's Garlic and Cheddar Biscuits! Now that is *brand-new* New South Cuisine. So, here you have the very recipe that was created for opening night, on November 7, 1997, at about four o'clock that afternoon. These biscuits literally became the first bite of food served from our new kitchen and they have been a highlight of the Soby's experience ever since."

ooooo

SOBY'S GARLIC AND CHEDDAR BISCUITS

(Makes 12 biscuits)

2 cups	Flour
1 Tbs	Baking Powder
1 tsp	Table Salt
1 tsp	Ground Nutmeg
1 Tbs	Granulated Garlic
½ cup	Shortening
½ cup	Sharp Yellow Cheddar Cheese, shredded
1 cup	Buttermilk
2 Tbs	Paprika
1 Tbs	Kosher Salt
1 Tbs	Granulated Garlic
4 Tbs	Butter, melted

Preheat the oven to 400°F and grease a baking pan. Place the flour, baking powder, table salt, nutmeg, and garlic into a food processor. Add the shortening, and using the pulse button, work the shortening into the dry ingredients until they become crumbly. Transfer the mixture into a bowl and mix in the buttermilk with your hands. Do not overwork the dough. Drop the dough from an ice cream scoop onto the greased baking pan. Bake for 10 minutes or until golden brown.

Mix the paprika, kosher salt, and garlic together and reserve. When the biscuits come out of the oven, brush them with the melted butter and sprinkle lightly with the spice mixture.

May 4, 2006

First meeting with Greenville Family Partnership, physicians, and restaurateurs about smoking ban. City Council would eventually pass an ordinance to go into effect January 2007

May 19, 2006

Carl inaugurated to National Restaurant Association Board during first meeting of NRA show in Chicago, as representative from South Carolina

September 3, 2006

Greenville resident, George Hincapie, wins USA Cycling Pro Championships in Greenville

THE SOBY'S WAY: FOOD AND WINE

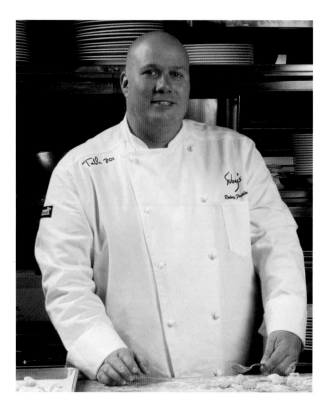

Rodney: "Ten years have passed since we opened Soby's. So many loyal guests and friends have requested recipes that we decided it was finally time to publish our first cookbook. But don't jump to the recipes just yet. We thought it might be helpful to say a few words about what you'll find there—why we chose the recipes we included, what 'The New South Pantry' section is all about, and how we hope you'll use this book."

Danny: "And since wine has been an important part of the 'Soby's Way' from the beginning, we've included pairing suggestions for every recipe. Chef Rodney will tell you about our food first, and then I'll be back with a few hints for how to make the best use of our recommendations for matching wines and other beverages to our recipes."

September 21, 2006

Soby's team travels to Washington, DC, to prepare and serve lunch to Senator Jim DeMint's Republican colleagues

September 22-24, 2006

First annual Southern Exposure, presented by the Cliffs, with proceeds going to charity foundation, Local Boys Do Good, for distribution to local causes

October 7, 2006

George Clooney dines at Restaurant O, as Clooney's team does a site visit for filming *Leatherheads* in the Greenville area

The recipes we've chosen fall into three categories. The first category is our "classics," signature dishes and popular favorites. These are the menu items that immediately come to mind when our regular guests think about the restaurant—Fried Green Tomato Napoleon, New Orleans BBQ Shrimp, and White Chocolate Banana Cream Pie, to name a few.

In the next category are dishes we think really exemplify "New South Cuisine." For example, you'll find our Smoked Chicken and Collard Greens Spring Roll. For this dish, we took an Asian idea and flavor profile but applied it to Southern ingredients. We did the same thing with our Sweet Potato Gnocchi, where we used sweet potatoes, sage, and pecans to produce a New South dish inspired by the Italian-style dumplings.

Then, there are some recipes we created just for the cookbook, which haven't even been on the menu yet. These include the Braised Duck Leg with Chipotle BBQ Sauce on a Sweet Potato Biscuit, as well as the Farm Raised South Carolina Striped Bass in Green Tomato Nage.

The New South Pantry section of the book briefly describes some of the important ingredients used in our kitchen, ranging from basics, such as salt and pepper, to regional products from our favorite producers. Whenever possible, we provide a Web site for you to obtain the items or to learn more about them.

Be market driven and choose the freshest and ripest ingredients available.

Some of the ingredients we use are produced in the Carolinas, but you can substitute items available "in your neck of the woods." The only thing we ask is that you think like a chef. Be market driven and choose the freshest and ripest ingredients available. Treat them thoughtfully and carefully. For example, make sure to keep meats and fish as cold as you can, even while you work with them. Be sure to serve the hot recipes hot, not at room temperature. If you choose to make any hot dishes in advance, cool them quickly in the refrigerator and heat them again thoroughly before serving.

You will find that most of the ingredients in this book are to be purchased fresh. There are exceptions; one is dry herbs. We often use dry herbs and spices if we are searing them quickly, as in an herb crust for meat or fish, or if they will be used in a long cooking process.

Most of the recipes in the Starters, Soups and Salads, Small Plates, and Entrées sections are portioned for six people. These quantities allow the right amount for families of three or four (with some leftovers or "chef's midnight suppers") or for couples who are cooking for guests. If you need to adjust the quantities slightly for more or fewer people, you can scale these recipes up or down as needed. Just be sure to taste as you go and season at the end to make sure you didn't lose any flavor along the way. Remember that cooking is an art and baking is a science. The

November 9-15, 2006
Teryi Youngblood, pastry chef at Soby's on the Side, spends a week working in Washington, DC, with David Guas

December 15, 2006
Court Square Restaurant Group closes on property for The Lazy Goat at 170 River Place

January 11, 2007
Twenty-fifth anniversary for Greenville's Hyatt Regency Hotel

Desserts have varying yields that make sense for each recipe. For best results, follow the dessert recipes carefully and don't make any adjustments.

Before we start cooking, there are just a few more things you need to know about using this book. When butter is called for in a recipe, always use unsalted, sweet cream butter. This allows the most control when it comes to seasoning a dish.

There is really no such thing as cooking wine. If you see the word *cooking* on a wine label, run! Cooking wines are salted and will change the flavor of the dish. You don't have to cook with the most expensive wine, but remember the general rule—if you wouldn't drink it, don't cook with it. Most of the recipes don't call for very much wine, so just use some of the wine you plan on drinking that night.

In our recipes we use certain terms to describe the cut sizes and shapes. Here is what we intend for each: *Minced* refers to an item that needs to be cut as small as possible. *Finely diced* means cut into about ⅟₁₆" x ⅟₁₆" cubes. *Diced* should be cut into approximately ¼" x ¼" cubes. For larger pieces, we use the word "cubed." *Cubed* usually refers to foods that will be cooked and puréed, so exact size isn't critical. However, the pieces should be about the same size so they cook evenly.

Throughout the book are occasional sections called the "Chef's Notebook." When you see this section in a recipe you are planning to make, please read it before shopping for ingredients.

The Chef's Notebook gives helpful suggestions on purchasing, timing, tools, and techniques needed for the preparation. We developed and tested the recipes using measurements typical in the home and quantities usually found in the grocery store.

So we hope we have achieved several goals in writing this book. First, we wanted to provide you with a casual, conversational insight to the Soby's "No-Walls" experience. And since you cannot be in our restaurant every night, our second goal was to allow you to be as well-fed and comfortable in your own home as we hope you have been in ours. For these reasons, the language used in the introductions, New South Pantry, and Chef's Notebook sections is informal yet helpful, as though we were with you while you are preparing these dishes at home. We refrained from using too many French culinary terms that make up our typical "kitchen lingo." Finally, we hope the book is a celebration of the hard work, dedication, and overall hospitality of the Soby's team, past and present.

We hope you have a great time making these dishes and sharing them with your family and friends.

Enjoy!

Chef Rodney

January 24, 2007

David and Carl team up with Stewart Spinks to make Devereaux's part of the Court Square Restaurant Group family

January 30, 2007

Chef Steven Devereaux Greene of Devereaux's hosts dinner at the James Beard House in New York

March 8, 2007

Bruce Cohn, manager of The Doobie Brothers and founder of B.R. Cohn Winery comes to Devereaux's for wine tasting before The Doobie Brothers concert at Peace Center

From the beginning, when Frank Kapp established Soby's wine program, wine has been important to all of us. His infectious passion for wine affected me so much that when he chose to pursue a new career path, I jumped at the chance to make the move from server to wine director. We were one of the first restaurants in Greenville to win a *Wine Spectator* "Award of Excellence." I'm pleased to say we currently hold the *Wine Spectator* "Best of Award of Excellence"—which the magazine describes as "clearly exceeding the requirements of the Award of Excellence, displaying vintage depth or excellent breadth across several wine regions." Early on we began building relationships with local wine enthusiasts, even future enthusiasts, by conducting wine tastings. Eventually, we were hosting multi-course wine dinners to sold-out crowds, featuring esteemed winemakers as guest speakers.

So, it was only natural for us to offer pairing suggestions—wines we have found work well with the dishes included in this book. However, as Chef Rodney said in his introduction to the recipes, don't be afraid to substitute. If you have a favorite wine you think will go well with a dish, try it and let your palate be the judge.

Now, here are just a few hints for understanding and using our pairing suggestions.

If you have a favorite wine you think will go well with a dish, try it and let your palate be the judge.

First, we needed to recommend either a wine made from white grapes, such as Chardonnay and Riesling, or a wine made from red grapes, for example, Pinot Noir and Syrah. By choosing the right varietal, the flavors of both the food and the wine are elevated and neither is overwhelmed.

Once we've determined the varietal, next comes the style. In many of our suggestions, we use the terms "New World" and "Old World." If these terms are unfamiliar, by Old World we mean Europe—primarily France, Italy, Spain, Germany, Austria—countries that have been making wine for centuries. These wines offer a sense of place—what the French call *terroir*. You might say, "Place equals taste." By New World, we are referring to the United States, Australia, New Zealand, South Africa, Chile, and Argentina. New World wines tend to put more emphasis on the fruit. You'll enjoy big, ripe fruit flavors, without necessarily having a clear sense of place.

Historically, wine enthusiasts thought Old World wines tended to be better with food, while New World wines were better for sipping alone. Like most generalizations, this is not necessarily true, but it does underscore the difference in style. When we make a broad recommendation for an Old World or New World wine, we mean most wine made in the style of that region will work with the

---

March 29, 2007

Chocolate Soiree at Greenville Country Club. Soby's Pastry Chef Teryi Youngblood wins two awards

April 20, 2007

First event in The Lazy Goat, Chris Fay and Kasey Cooper rehearsal dinner. Food by Table 301 Catering, as kitchen is not yet ready in new space

June 18, 2007

The Lazy Goat opens to the public, directed by Chef Lindsay Autry and Table 301 Manager Aimee Maher

dish. Occasionally, we found it necessary to be more specific; for example, recommendations such as Bordeaux and Burgundy in the Old World or Sonoma and Carneros in the New World. We only recommend these fairly narrow designations when we think those wines offer something very specific to complement the recipe. In those cases, we've included a descriptive note explaining why.

With desserts particularly, our goal is to prompt you to try some interesting pairings you might not have considered. Certainly, coffee, tea, or espresso go well with most desserts. But a glass of Port or a sip of *limoncello* may turn an already wonderful dessert into a completely extraordinary experience. After-dinner drinks are a well-established part of the meal in countries that have great culinary tradition, and for good reason! So remember that with a very special meal, the "wine program" ought to continue all the way through dessert.

Finally, the mention of limoncello in the previous paragraph should alert you that not every pairing suggestion is limited to wine. Some recipes— barbeque or spicy foods, for example—almost cry out for beer! Although it is possible to successfully pair wines with almost anything, some recipes include other options as well.

Just as we expect Soby's "New South Cuisine" to evolve in the future, we intend to continue adding exciting new wines from new parts of the world to our Wine List. To our many long-time friends and wine enthusiasts, thank you for your support. And for those who have not yet dined with us, I hope to see you in the restaurant soon.

Cheers!

Danny Baker

Danny Baker

August 14, 2007

Tiger Woods announces plans to design and build his first golf course in the US with Jim Anthony and The Cliffs Communities

September 14-16, 2007

Second annual Southern Exposure featuring Chef Thomas Keller, The French Laundry; Pastry Chef David Guas, Damgoodsweet Consulting Group; Michael McDonald, Branford Marsalis, and Edwin McCain

November 4, 2007

Soby's Tenth Anniversary Party

Starters

40 · Crispy Fried Calamari
Creole Sauce, Tomato Horseradish Tartar

44 · Grilled Vegetable Stack
Split Creek Farm Goat Cheese, Tomato Basil Coulis, Tapenade Crouton

46 · Smoked Port Royal Shrimp
Roasted Sweet Corn Cake, Jalapeño Apple Butter

51 · Fried Green Tomato Napoleon
Jalapeño Pimiento Cheese, Sweet and Sour Greens, Roasted Red Pepper Coulis

**57 · Smoked Chicken and Collard Greens
Spring Roll**
Mustard Green Coulis, Pepper Jelly

60 · Spinach and Artichoke Dip
Garlic Herb Bruschetta

63 · Clemson Blue Cheese Fondue
Blackened Blue Crab, Hand Cut Potato Chips

66 · Crispy Chicken Livers
Caramelized Red Onion Jam, Applewood Smoked Bacon "Red Eye" Gravy

70 · Baked Oysters
Andouille Sausage, Collard Greens,
Crawfish Tails, Creole Tomato Hollandaise

Crispy Fried Calamari
Creole Sauce, Tomato Horseradish Tartar

(Serves 6)

Creole Sauce:

2 Tbs	Olive Oil
1 cup	Yellow Onion, diced
½ cup	Green Bell Pepper, diced
½ cup	Celery, diced
¼ cup	Scallions, thinly sliced
¼ cup	Fresh Garlic, minced
2 Tbs	Soby's Creole Seasoning, see page 204
1 cup	Fresh Roma Tomatoes, diced
56 oz	Diced Tomatoes (canned)

Tartar:

28 oz	Diced Tomatoes (canned)
½ cup	Prepared Horseradish
1 tsp	Fresh Garlic, minced
2 cups	Mayonnaise
1 tsp	Lemon Juice, freshly squeezed
2 tsp	Salt

"At Soby's the most popular appetizers have always been the ones that can be sampled by everyone, whether business associates or family members. Calamari works well for sharing. All parents know that children eat only chicken fingers and macaroni and cheese when they go out. You will be surprised to find that kids also love this appetizer. I like to send an order of calamari to the table and watch from the kitchen as the parents are amazed because their children can't get enough of the tasty squid."

For the Creole Sauce: In a large saucepan over medium-high heat, sauté the onion, pepper, and celery in the olive oil until the vegetables are soft and lightly browned. Add the scallions and garlic and continue to cook for 2 minutes, stirring often so the garlic doesn't burn. Add the creole seasoning, stir, and cook for 2 more minutes. Add the tomatoes and bring the sauce to a simmer. Reduce the heat and simmer for 15 to 20 minutes. Purée the sauce slightly with an immersion blender, leaving it a little chunky. Serve hot.

For the Tartar: Empty the canned tomatoes into a lint-free cloth, such as cheesecloth or a clean linen napkin. Bring the corners together around the tomatoes and gently twist to enclose the tomatoes in a pouch. Continue to twist until the liquid is squeezed out of the tomatoes. Place the tomatoes and all other ingredients into a food processor and process until well combined. Refrigerate until needed. →

Calamari:

	Vegetable Oil
2 lbs	Calamari Tubes and Tentacles, cleaned
2 cups	Flour
	Salt and Fresh Ground Black Pepper

For the Calamari: Heat the oil in a pot or a portable fryer to 350°F. Make sure the oil is at least 6 inches from the top of the pot to allow space for adding the calamari and to prevent the oil from boiling over.

Cut the calamari tubes (bodies) into rings approximately ½ inch wide. If the tentacle portions are big, cut them in half so they can be eaten in one bite. While cutting the pieces, remove any stray pieces of cartilage.

Measure the flour into a shallow container. Place the calamari in a bowl and cover with water (the water helps the flour stick to the calamari). Remove a handful of calamari from the water and quickly put it into the flour. Shake off any excess flour and carefully drop the calamari into the oil. After about 10 seconds, gently stir the calamari (or shake it if using a fryer basket) to make sure the pieces do not stick together. After 45 seconds, lift the calamari out of the oil and allow any excess oil to drip back into the pot or fryer. Drain on a plate lined with paper towels. Repeat until all calamari is cooked. Serve hot.

Finish the Dish: Place the cooked calamari in a bowl and season with salt and pepper. Serve hot with creole sauce and tartar on the side.

Pairing Suggestions: Pilsner-style beer or a dry sparkling rosé wine. Bubbles, whether in beer or sparkling wine, go well with most fried foods.

Chef's Notebook

The trick for successfully frying calamari is to have the oil at the right temperature and fry the calamari quickly without dropping the temperature of the oil by overloading the pot.

The other important detail is not to overwhelm the delicate seafood with a heavy breading. Just a dusting with flour is perfect.

In this recipe, you can (and should) make the creole sauce as much as three or four days ahead and keep it refrigerated until needed. Make the tartar as much as one week ahead. Then on the night you serve the dish, properly cooking the squid is the only thing you have to worry about.

Table 301 at Soby's

A No-Walls Welcome

DAVID: "In 1997 when we were designing Soby's, open kitchens were still a new trend. No walls, guests able to see into the kitchen, maybe even a Chef's Table—that was all the rage. But the thing is, Carl and I had seen a lot of restaurants in which there were still invisible walls between the staff and the guests, between the servers and the kitchen, between the owners and the staff. We didn't want any walls. That's why we built this kitchen just the way you see it. Every table above the kitchen is a Chef's Table. We didn't want to close in the kitchen, separating ourselves and the staff from our guests. Complete transparency—that was the goal. We want what-you-see to be what-you-get, in the best and broadest sense of that phrase."

CARL: "That philosophy led us to name the parent company of our restaurants 'Table 301.' At Soby's, Table 301 sits directly above the kitchen. The guests can see the chef. The chef can see the guests. Servers link the two. Every guest should feel as comfortable at Soby's as if they were sitting with friends in a big kitchen at home. We sometimes kid ourselves about offering guests the *Cheers* experience—'everybody knows your name and they're always glad you came.' But that feeling is really what we're all about. Our goal is a complete no-walls welcome."

Grilled Vegetable Stack
Split Creek Farm Goat Cheese, Tomato Basil Coulis, Tapenade Crouton

(Serves 6)

Coulis:

12	Roma Tomatoes
2 Tbs	Olive Oil
⅓ cup	Shallot, minced
2 tsp	Fresh Garlic, minced
12	Fresh Basil Leaves
1 Tbs	Salt
Pinch	Fresh Ground Black Pepper
½ cup	Olive Oil

Crouton:

1 cup	Kalamata Olives, pitted
2	Anchovy Filets
1 Tbs	Capers, drained
1 tsp	Fresh Garlic, minced
2 Tbs	Olive Oil
2 Tbs	Italian Parsley, chopped
1	French Baguette
	Olive Oil

Vegetables:

½ cup	Balsamic Vinegar
1 tsp	Fresh Garlic, minced
1 tsp	Worcestershire Sauce
½ cup	Olive Oil
1	Zucchini
2	Yellow Squash
2	Japanese Eggplant
6	Portobello Mushroom Caps
1	Red Onion (large)
2	Roma Tomatoes
	Salt and Fresh Ground Black Pepper
8 oz	Split Creek Farm Goat Cheese, at room temperature

"Hello summer! Don't feel it is necessary to use exactly the vegetables listed in the recipe. Whatever your favorite summer vegetables are will work great. Have fun!"

For the Coulis: Remove and discard the stem end of the tomatoes and cut tomatoes in half lengthwise. Place in a bowl with the 2 tablespoons olive oil, tossing to coat. Place the tomatoes on a hot grill and cook until softened and the skin is caramelized (browned), about 5 minutes. Sauté the shallot and garlic in a small amount of olive oil until soft, but not brown. Place all ingredients except the remaining ½ cup olive oil in a blender and blend on high speed until smooth. Drizzle in the remaining olive oil as you blend. Serve hot.

For the Crouton: Begin by preparing the tapenade. Place the olives, anchovies, capers, and garlic in a food processor and process until the ingredients are finely chopped. Drizzle in the 2 tablespoons olive oil while processing. Stir in the parsley.

Slice the bread diagonally ½ inch thick. Brush the bread with olive oil and place on a hot grill. Grill the bread on both sides being careful not to over-char the bread. Spread tapenade on each toast.

For the Vegetables: Whisk together the vinegar, garlic, Worcestershire sauce, and olive oil for the marinade. Slice all the vegetables except the mushrooms into ¼-inch thick slices on the diagonal. Carefully cut off the gills on the underside of each mushroom cap. Toss the vegetable slices and the mushroom caps with the marinade and sprinkle with salt and pepper. Place on a hot grill. When they have a nice golden grill mark, flip them and grill the other side. Remove to a platter and keep warm.

Finish the Dish: Ladle some of the coulis on a plate. Next, layer the vegetables to form a colorful stack. Top with goat cheese and a warm tapenade crouton.

Pairing Suggestion: Sancerre (French Sauvignon Blanc). This Old World selection complements the goat cheese and earthy flavors in this dish.

Smoked Port Royal Shrimp
Roasted Sweet Corn Cake, Jalapeño Apple Butter

(Serves 6 with some leftovers)

Apple Butter:

6	Granny Smith Apples
2	Jalapeños, seeded and finely diced
¼ cup	Maple Syrup
½ cup	Water
¼ lb	Butter
	Salt and Fresh Ground Black Pepper

Shrimp:

½ gallon	Water
1½ cups	Kosher Salt
½ cup	Sugar
¼ cup	Pickling Spice
1 clove	Fresh Garlic, peeled and smashed
1	Lemon, juiced
2 lbs	Port Royal Shrimp (21-25 ct), peeled and deveined

"The flavor combination of this dish will blow you away. You can also make this recipe as an hors d'oeuvre by baking the batter in mini muffin tins and topping the muffin with the apple butter and the shrimp."

For the Apple Butter: Peel and rough chop the apples removing the core and seeds. Place the jalapeños, apples, maple syrup, and water in a saucepan and cook on medium heat until the apples are quite tender. Purée the apple mixture in a blender. As the apples become smooth and while the mixture is still hot, add the butter in small batches, puréeing to emulsify. Season to taste with salt and pepper. Reserve until needed and serve warm or cold.

For the Shrimp: Combine all ingredients except the shrimp in a saucepan and bring to a boil. Remove from the heat and cool over an ice bath. When the brine is cool, add the shrimp and soak for 20 minutes. Drain the shrimp and pat dry with paper towels. Refrigerate the shrimp while you prepare the other components.

Smoke the shrimp in a smoker or on a grill for 5 minutes or until shrimp is just cooked through. →

Corn Cakes:

1 Tbs	Olive Oil
1 cup	Fresh Corn Kernels, removed from cob (about 2 ears)
¾ cup	Yellow Cornmeal
¾ cup	Flour
1 tsp	Table Salt
⅓ cup	Sugar
1½ tsp	Baking Powder
½ tsp	Cayenne Pepper
1½ cups	Milk
3	Eggs
2 Tbs	Butter, melted
	Vegetable Oil

For the Corn Cakes: Place a skillet on high heat and heat the olive oil just until it starts to smoke. Carefully add the corn kernels and cook them through, allowing them to brown lightly before stirring. Remove from the heat and reserve. Meanwhile, sift together the cornmeal, flour, salt, sugar, and baking powder in a large bowl. In another bowl, whisk together the milk, eggs, butter, and corn. Add the wet ingredients to the dry ingredients and stir to combine well. Allow the batter to rest for approximately 20 minutes, to allow the flour and cornmeal to soak up some of the liquid. Using a ¼-cup measure, drop the mixture onto a hot griddle or seasoned cast iron skillet with a small amount of oil. When the first side turns golden brown (about 2 minutes), flip the cakes and cook on the other side for about 1 minute, until the cakes are cooked through. The cakes should be thin, like crepes.

Finish the Dish: Take a warm cake and spread a little apple butter on one side. Fold it in half and then in half again to make a triangle shape. Spread a generous amount of the apple butter on a warm plate. Top with one of the stuffed cakes. Arrange six shrimp on the plate. Serve warm.

Pairing Suggestion: Viognier (Sonoma County or Paso Robles). The round fruitiness of Viognier is a perfect contrast to the smokiness of the dish.

Chef's Notebook

The most difficult thing about this dish is preparing the recipes so everything is ready at the same time. Here is my suggestion: Make the apple butter and the brine for the shrimp a couple of days in advance. Make the corn cake batter a couple of hours before you need it. When it is time to do the final cooking, brine the shrimp. While the shrimp are brining, make the corn cakes, cover them with a damp cloth, and stack them in a warm oven. Rinse the shrimp and pat them dry. Next, smoke the shrimp and place them in the warm oven while you assemble the corn cakes and arrange the plate. Add the shrimp and serve.

The chef always tries to provide a contrast of textures, flavors, and colors to a dish to make it interesting. Chefs are now adding temperature contrast to that combination. To add that contrast to this recipe, serve the apple butter cold and the corn cakes and shrimp hot.

Thank You for Smoking!

Smoking is undoubtedly one of the most popular cooking techniques in the South. No other preparation technique adds as much flavor to a dish. Smoking adds flavor by laying a thin film of smoke on top of the food item. Smoking for a longer period of time causes the smoked flavor to penetrate the food as well. There are two methods of smoking: cold smoking (used for bacon) and hot smoking (which cooks as it smokes). The recipes in this book use hot smoking.

The most effective tool for smoking is a smoker. If you have a smoker, use it according to the manufacturer's recommendations. If you don't have a smoker, here are some tips and methods.

Smoking Tips:
- Smoke only outside.
- In the Southeast, the most popular wood for smoking is hickory. You can buy chips at your local supermarket.
- If the food item is large, it may need to smoke for a long period of time. To control the amount of smoke and prevent the chips from burning up too fast, soak them in water first.
- If the food item is small, you do not need to soak the chips.

Charcoal Grill:
- Use hardwood charcoal whenever possible for maximum flavor.
- Heat the charcoal and allow it to burn down to a moderate temperature (so the charcoal does not flame up).
- Add a small handful of wood chips to the charcoal.
- Place the food on the grill and close the lid.
- Cook the food to the desired doneness.

Gas Grill:
- Heat the grill to medium-high.
- Put a small handful of wood smoking chips in an aluminum pie tin.
- Place the tin on one side of the grill grate.
- Close the grill cover and allow the chips to heat until they are smoking.
- Place the food on the grill and close the lid.
- Cook the food to the desired doneness.

Fried Green Tomato Napoleon
Jalapeño Pimiento Cheese, Sweet and Sour Greens, Roasted Red Pepper Coulis

(Serves 6 with plenty of extra pimiento cheese and greens)

Pimiento Cheese: (yields about 6 cups)

2 lbs	Sharp Yellow Cheddar Cheese, shredded
8 oz	Cream Cheese, at room temperature
7 oz	Diced Pimientos, drained
1	Jalapeño, seeded and finely diced
½ cup	Green Olives Stuffed with Pimientos, chopped
1 cup	Mayonnaise

Greens: (yields about 10 cups)

2 lbs	Collard Greens
2 lbs	Turnip Greens
2 lbs	Mustard Greens
2 Tbs	Olive Oil
2	Yellow Onions, cut into strips
½ cup	Fresh Garlic, chopped
1	Smoked Ham Hock (a smoked turkey leg also works)
2 cups	Apple Cider Vinegar
1 lb	Brown Sugar
8 cups	Chicken Stock
1 Tbs	Salt

"This item was on the first Soby's menu and has been on most of the menus since. One of the nice things about this recipe is you can use the various parts for different applications. For example, pimiento cheese is a staple in the Southern household. This recipe for it can be made up to one week in advance and is more than you need for the dish. The sweet and sour greens are also great in many preparations. As for the tomatoes, at the restaurant we fry them in a deep fat fryer. If you have one, by all means use it. The recipe here calls for shallow frying them in a sauté pan so equipment is not an issue."

For the Pimiento Cheese: Mix all ingredients together until well combined. Refrigerate until ready to serve.

For the Greens: Greens are naturally sandy and need to be cleaned carefully. Remove and discard the largest part of the stem from each leaf. Plunge the leaves into a sink full of cold water. Agitate the greens in the water and allow them to sit for 1 minute until the sediment settles to the bottom. Remove the greens from the dirty water. Rinse out the sink and repeat this process three times to make sure no sand remains on the greens.

In small bunches, roll up the leaves and cut into strips. Heat the olive oil in a large pot and sauté the onions until soft but not brown. Add the garlic and cook 2 more minutes (do not brown the garlic). Add the ham hock, vinegar, sugar, and stock. Bring to a boil. Add the greens a little at a time (don't worry that it seems like a lot of greens; they shrink considerably as they cook). When all the greens are in the pot, reduce the heat to a simmer and cook, covered, for 1 hour or until the greens are tender. Refrigerate the finished greens for up to one week. Warm in small amounts as needed. →

Coulis:

3	Red Bell Peppers
1 Tbs	Olive Oil
1 cup	Chicken Stock
½ cup	Olive Oil
1 Tbs	Cornstarch
¼ cup	Water
	Salt and Fresh Ground Black Pepper

Tomatoes:

3-4	Green Beefsteak Tomatoes
3	Eggs
1 cup	Milk
2 cups	Flour
4 cups	Golden Dipt® Breader
	Vegetable Oil
	Salt

For the Coulis: Lightly coat the peppers with the 1 tablespoon olive oil. Place the peppers on a hot grill (or in a 500°F oven) and char the outside completely. Remove the peppers from the heat and immediately put them in a bowl and cover with plastic wrap. The steaming process that takes place as the peppers cool helps release the skin from the flesh. When the peppers are cool, rub the skins off. Remove the stem end and the seeds and rough chop the peppers. Put the chicken stock and the peppers in a saucepan and bring to a simmer. Mix the cornstarch with the water and whisk it into the sauce. Continue to simmer for 5 minutes. Remove mixture from the heat and pour it into a blender. Blend on high, drizzling in the ½ cup olive oil. Season to taste with salt and pepper. Serve hot.

For the Tomatoes: Slice off and discard the top and bottom of each tomato. Slice the tomatoes into 18 ¼-inch thick slices. Whisk together the eggs and milk to make an egg wash. Dust the tomato slices with flour and tap off the excess. Place the slices, a few at a time, into the egg wash. Then coat the slices with Golden Dipt. Pour vegetable oil into a skillet to about 1 inch deep. Heat oil on medium-high heat until it sizzles when a small amount of flour is dropped in. Fry the tomato slices in small batches, until they turn golden brown and crisp. Flip and fry on the other side the same way. Remove the cooked tomatoes to a plate lined with paper towels. Season the tomatoes with salt and place in a warm oven until all tomatoes are cooked.

Finish the Dish: Ladle some of the coulis around the plate. Stack three tomatoes, spreading pimiento cheese between the layers. Place three piles of greens around each plate. Serve hot.

Pairing Suggestion: Albariño (a unique Spanish white varietal). Albariño's acidity serves the same function as bubbles with fried food, keeping your palate fresh.

The entertaining kitchen in The Loft at Soby's   Photo by Mark Lamkin

THE LOFT AT SOBY'S

DAVID: "When we transformed the Cancellation Shoe Mart into Soby's, we thought we had a lot more space than we needed. For example, we didn't plan to open the mezzanine over the kitchen right away. But guest response demanded it. For a month after the restaurant opened, we spent our days frantically converting the mezzanine into dining space, while serving guests downstairs at night.

Danny Baker, Wine Director and host at The Loft

We boarded up the two-story L-shaped wing on the back of the restaurant while we conceptualized what to do with it. We heard it had been storage for buggies and wagons in the late 1800s, and served as a warehouse for Jones Furniture and the Cancellation Shoe Mart."

CARL: "What the upstairs part of the L-shaped wing became is what we started out calling 'The Corporate Apartment' and today refer to as 'The Loft.' Our original plan was to do what a lot of other property owners along Main Street had done: create retail space on the ground floor with residential space up above. We designed two apartments that we planned to lease as downtown lofts.

"But around the same time, an event planner with General Electric phoned us about hosting

Artifacts from restoration of The Loft, including bottles from the building's use as Dispensary #1, as well as bank checks from Jones Furniture

*The custom-made table
in the dining room can
seat up to 20 guests*
Photo by Mark Lamkin

a private dinner for 30 people on a Sunday night. Jack Welch, the CEO of General
Electric, was coming to town for an important business dinner. Since the dinner was
to be held on Sunday night, when Soby's is normally closed, GE could have had the
restaurant all to themselves. We would have transformed it into whatever they wanted.

"We gave that proposal our best shot and knew that GE's execs would love our
food. But the next thing we heard was that they had chosen another venue, a sterile
'banquet room' in a local fine dining restaurant. Boy, were we disappointed!

"Well, it just so happened that David and I learned this news minutes before a
meeting with our architects to review their final design of the apartments. Sitting in that
meeting, I was lost in thought over what we could have done to win the bid for that
dinner. I knew why we'd lost it: we didn't have a 'private dining room.'

"As we were sitting there, I heard the architects refer to an 'entertaining kitchen'
in their design and something just clicked. We would not divide the space into two
units. We would create one large apartment, laid-out for entertaining—a private dining
room like no one in Greenville had seen. We would provide a personal chef for every
event, decorate the space with the finest furnishings, install the best possible bedding,
and offer it to guests as the 'world's smallest luxury hotel.'"

DAVID: "And that was it. We changed the design and never looked back. The rest, as
they say, is history. The Loft continues to be one of Greenville's favorite entertaining
venues and we have hosted such celebrities as Hillary Clinton, Kurt Russell, John
O'Hurley, George Hincapie, and many more."

Smoked Chicken and Collard Greens Spring Roll

Mustard Green Coulis, Pepper Jelly

(Makes 12 large or 24 small)

"The flavors for this dish were directly inspired by many trips to local Chinese restaurants, where Chef David and I satisfy cravings for crisp spring rolls dipped in both spicy Chinese mustard and sweet duck sauce. Here the mustard greens make a beautifully colorful replacement for the Chinese mustard and the sweetness of the pepper jelly is better than any duck sauce we've ever had."

Spring Roll:

1½ lbs	Boneless, Skinless Chicken Thighs (4-6)
	Salt and Fresh Ground Black Pepper
	Hickory Wood Chips
2	Red Bell Peppers, roasted, peeled, and seeded
2 cups	Sweet and Sour Greens, see recipe, page 51
1	Egg
1 Tbs	Water
24	Spring Roll Wrappers (do not open until needed)
	Cornstarch
	Vegetable Oil

For the Spring Roll: Season the chicken thighs with salt and pepper and smoke with the hickory wood chips in an outdoor smoker or a grill until chicken is cooked (see the method on page 49). Remove the chicken from the smoker and cut it into small cubes. Dice the roasted peppers and add to the chicken. Place the greens in the center of a lint-free towel or a piece of cheesecloth. Draw the corners together and twist the ends tightly, pushing the liquid out of the greens. When the greens are dry, give them a rough chop and add them to the chicken and peppers. Refrigerate the filling until cool. Squeeze out excess liquid before using the filling.

Whisk together the egg and the water to make an egg wash.

To make the rolls, unwrap the spring roll wrappers and lay out one on the counter so one of the corners is pointing toward you (diamond shape). Brush a small amount of egg wash in the top corner. Place ⅓ cup filling in the bottom corner for a large roll and half of that for an hors d'oeuvre size roll. Roll the wrapper tightly around the filling. Halfway through the roll, fold the left and right corners tightly to the center and continue rolling away from you until you have a tightly wrapped spring roll. For the large spring rolls, wrap each one again using the same method so they are double wrapped. The second wrapper prevents the roll from becoming soggy. As you finish each spring roll, dust it lightly with cornstarch. Continue making rolls until the filling is gone.

Heat the oil in a fryer to 350°F. Fry the spring rolls in small batches for approximately 3 minutes for the large ones and 1½ to 2 minutes for the small ones. Drain on paper towels. →

Coulis:

1 lb	Mustard Greens
1 cup	Apple Cider Vinegar
½ cup	Onion, diced
2 Tbs	Brown Sugar
2 cloves	Fresh Garlic, chopped
1 Tbs	Cornstarch
¼ cup	Water
½ cup	Olive Oil
	Salt

Pepper Jelly:

1	Jalapeño, seeded and finely diced
1	Red Bell Pepper, finely diced
1	Yellow Bell Pepper, finely diced
1 cup	Apple Cider Vinegar
½ cup	Water
2 cups	Sugar
½ cup	Cilantro Leaves, chopped

For the Coulis: Greens are naturally sandy and need to be cleaned carefully. Remove and discard the largest part of the stem from each leaf. Plunge the leaves into a sink full of cold water. Agitate the greens in the water and allow them to sit for 1 minute until the sediment settles to the bottom. Remove the greens from the dirty water. Rinse out the sink and repeat this process three times to make sure no sand remains on the greens.

Next, combine the vinegar, onion, sugar, and garlic in a small saucepan. Bring the mixture to a simmer and reduce by half. Mix the cornstarch with the water and whisk into the simmering liquid. Continue to simmer, stirring constantly for 1 minute. Chill the reduction by placing it in a bowl over an ice bath. Place the greens and the vinegar reduction in a blender and blend on high until smooth. While still blending, drizzle in the olive oil slowly to emulsify. Season to taste with salt and refrigerate until needed.

For the Pepper Jelly: Put all ingredients except the cilantro in a saucepan and bring to a simmer. Allow the mixture to simmer for approximately 1 hour or until the liquid has thickened to a light syrup consistency. Remove from the heat and stir in the cilantro. Cool the mixture and store in the refrigerator until needed. The syrup thickens more as it cools.

Finish the Dish: Arrange the spring rolls on a plate with the coulis and pepper jelly. Allow one large roll per person for an appetizer, or two smaller ones as an hors d'oeuvre.

Pairing Suggestions: Riesling or Gewürztraminer (New or Old World). These varietals are a perfect complement to Asian food because the slight amount of residual sugar in the wine offsets the spiciness. Don't specifically seek out a sweet wine. Just buy a typical, almost-dry Riesling or Gewürztraminer.

Chef's Notebook

This recipe is great as an appetizer before a meal, but it may even be better as an hors d'oeuvre for a cocktail party. You can make a bunch of the rolls, place them on a baking sheet, and put the sheet into the freezer. Once the rolls are frozen, remove them from the baking sheet and put them in a plastic freezer bag in the freezer until you need them. They will last several months and can be ready quickly—great for when guests unexpectedly show up.

COOKING AT THE JAMES BEARD HOUSE

The mission of the James Beard Foundation in New York is "To celebrate, preserve, and nurture America's culinary heritage and diversity in order to elevate the appreciation of our culinary excellence." One of the ways they accomplish this mission is by staging dinners at the Beard House, presented by visiting chefs from around the world. The Beard House is the actual home where Chef Beard (considered by many to be the father of American gastronomy) lived. The house was preserved after Beard's

New South Cuisine in New York

death in 1985 thanks to the vision of Beard's long-time friend, Chef Julia Child, famous for her cookbooks—especially *Mastering the Art of French Cooking*—and perhaps even more so for her television series, *The French Chef*.

DAVID: "In January 2000, we were invited to cook at the James Beard House in New York. To cook at the Beard House is an honor for any chef. Of course, for us Southern boys, we didn't really think about the dinner being held in January. So it was—ahh, a little daunting—as all of us arrived in New York in the middle of a blizzard. But the Beard House welcome was warm and the dinner was sold-out."

RODNEY: "One of our most special memories of the Beard House dinner involves running into Jean-Louis Palladin. I had been a fan of Chef Palladin for years. In 1974 Jean-Louis was the youngest French chef ever to win two Michelin stars. When he came to America in 1979, he studied—and then helped improve the quality of—local ingredients for fine dining nationwide. So who do David and I almost bowl over, as we are piling out of a cab in New York City? Jean-Louis Palladin! When he died the next year at age 55, the culinary world lost a great teacher, a passionate chef, and an extraordinarily gracious man.

"To illustrate just how gracious, during the quick encounter David and I had with Jean-Louis, we mentioned that we had plans to eat in his friend's restaurant, Citronelle in Washington, DC, on our way back to South Carolina. When we arrived at the restaurant, Michel Richard (as esteemed as Jean-Louis in both France and America) walked straight over to us and said, 'My friend Jean-Louis called and said that he had friends coming down and that I should take good care of you.'

"But perhaps the best memory for me of the Beard House dinner was that Damian, my brother, flew up from Florida to attend. He had done a James Beard dinner previously with one of the chefs from Disney. He had clued us in what a nice touch it would be to bring the dinner guests a gift. That's when we put together the CD of Carolina music, along with the menu and the photos of South Carolina."

CARL: "The Beard House dinner was a great feeling for all of us, to have the opportunity to represent Greenville's rapidly emerging food scene to a New York audience. For David, Rod, and Frank Kapp to arrive in the middle of a nor'easter and pull off a dinner that garnered rave reviews, was an incredible accomplishment—and one that made us all very proud."

Spinach and Artichoke Dip
Garlic Herb Bruschetta

(Makes 2 quarts; serves 12 for hors d'oeuvres)

Dip:

4 cups	Artichoke Hearts (canned)
1 lb	Fresh Spinach, stems removed
2 tsp	Fresh Garlic, minced
2 cups	Mayonnaise
2 cups	Parmesan Cheese, grated
1 tsp	Crushed Red Pepper Flakes (optional)
3	Roma Tomatoes, sliced

Bruschetta:

1 Tbs	Fresh Garlic, minced
½ bunch	Italian Parsley, stems removed, finely chopped
½ cup	Parmesan Cheese, grated
1 cup	Olive Oil
1 loaf	French Bread (baguette)
	Salt

"Almost every time I go to a party, I hear someone say, 'I hope you brought Soby's spinach and artichoke dip.' Now you can make it for your parties, too. At Soby's we serve the dip hot, but it is also very good cold."

For the Dip: Preheat oven to 350°F. Drain the artichoke hearts, rough chop small, and place them in a large bowl. Wash the spinach thoroughly to remove any sand. Blanch the spinach for 10 seconds and shock (see method on page 131). Remove excess liquid from the spinach by squeezing it in a piece of cheesecloth or a lint-free towel. Rough chop the spinach and add it to the artichokes. Add the remaining ingredients, except the tomatoes, and mix well. Transfer the dip to a 2-qt casserole dish and garnish with tomato slices. Bake uncovered until the dip is bubbly and hot in the middle, approximately 45 minutes.

For the Bruschetta: Combine the garlic, parsley, and Parmesan cheese in a food processor. With the processor running, drizzle in the olive oil. Slice the bread into ½-inch thick rounds. Spread the garlic-parsley mix liberally on each round. Sprinkle with salt. Bake in a 350°F oven until the edges of the bread are crisp and the topping is golden brown, about 5 minutes.

Finish the Dish: Serve the hot dip with hot garlic herb bruschetta.

Pairing Suggestion: Pinot Grigio (Italy). Pinot Grigio makes a wonderful welcome wine for events in your home and works well with the garlic and other Mediterranean components of this dish.

Clemson Blue Cheese Fondue
Blackened Blue Crab, Hand Cut Potato Chips

(Serves 6)

"At Soby's we really love *the artisanal blue cheese made at Clemson University (see the New South Pantry). Our signature Blue Cheese Fondue made with Blackened Blue Crab is great served with homemade hand cut potato chips. There is something about homemade potato chips that gives people the warm fuzzies. The ingredient list is quite simple, but the method is what makes the difference between crisp or soggy chips."*

Chips:

2 lbs	Idaho Potatoes
	Vegetable Oil
	Salt

For the Chips: Scrub potatoes under cold running water with a brush to remove all dirt from the skin. Slice the potatoes $\frac{1}{16}$ inch thick using a v-slicer or mandoline and put them immediately into a container of hot water. Stir to separate the slices and let them sit in the hot water for 10 minutes. Place the container in the sink and run cold water over the slices. Stir the slices again to separate them. Keep running the cold water over them until the water turns clear.

Meanwhile, heat vegetable oil in a deep fat fryer or in a tall pot to 350°F. Remove a handful of potato slices from the water and pat dry with paper towels. Gently drop the potatoes into the hot oil. Carefully stir the chips to keep them separated. When the chips have turned golden brown and are crisp, about 5 minutes, carefully remove them to a baking sheet lined with paper towels and season lightly with salt. Allow the oil a couple of minutes to return to temperature and drop in another handful of potato slices. Repeat until all the chips are fried. Serve hot.

To use the chips later, keep the chips uncovered until they are completely cool, then cover them with plastic wrap or place them in an airtight bag, being careful not to crush them. To refresh the chips, place them on a baking sheet in a 400°F oven for 1 to 2 minutes before serving. →

Fondue:

¼ tsp	Olive Oil
½ tsp	Fresh Garlic, minced
1 cup	White Wine
1 cup	Chicken Stock
1 pint	Heavy Cream
1 lb	Clemson Blue Cheese, crumbled
1 Tbs	Cornstarch
½ cup	Water

Crab:

1 lb	Backfin Crabmeat
1 Tbs	Soby's Creole Seasoning, see page 204
	Vegetable Oil

For the Fondue: Cook the garlic in a sauté pan with the olive oil until the garlic softens and lends its flavor to the oil, but do not brown the garlic. Add the wine and chicken stock and simmer until the liquid is reduced by half. Add the cream and simmer until the liquid is reduced by half again. Using an immersion blender, incorporate the blue cheese. Bring the liquid back to a simmer. Meanwhile, combine the water and cornstarch to make a slurry. When the fondue is simmering again, drizzle in the slurry and stir until the fondue is thick enough to coat the back of a spoon.

For the Crab: Pick through the crabmeat and remove any bits of shell, taking care not to shred the crabmeat. Toss the crab with the spice mix. Heat a small amount of oil in a nonstick skillet to the smoking point and add the crabmeat. Allow the crab to sit for 1 minute and sear. Flip or stir the crabmeat and sear again.

Finish the Dish: Pour the blackened crab on top of the hot blue cheese fondue. Serve with warm potato chips. Top with a sprinkling of creole seasoning if desired.

Pairing Suggestion: Prosecco (Italy). The bubbles and the fruitiness of the Prosecco complement the salt on the chips and in the blue cheese.

Chef's Notebook

Soby's chefs are highly trained and experienced in using cutlery. However, when it comes to thinly sliced produce, the skill of the chef can rarely top the precision of a sharp mandoline. As I tell my new apprentices, you will not teach the mandoline respect; it will teach you. Use it carefully and realize that when slicing potato chips is no time to multitask.

When it comes to blackening food, learn from Chef David's mistake. Done properly, blackening sends out quite a bit of smoke into the kitchen (and the living room, and the bathroom, the bedrooms... you get the picture). Make sure the kitchen is well ventilated, or do that part of the recipe outside. If neither is possible, go ahead and sauté the crab at a lower heat, but realize the food will not achieve the same depth of flavor.

Crispy Chicken Livers
Caramelized Red Onion Jam, Applewood Smoked Bacon "Red Eye" Gravy

(Serves 6)

Onion Jam:

3 cups	Red Onions, diced
1 cup	Red Wine
1 cup	Sugar
1 cup	Dried Cranberries
1	Orange
½ cup	Grenadine

Gravy:

1 cup	Applewood Smoked Bacon, diced
½ cup	Yellow Onion, diced
1 Tbs	Flour
1 cup	Black Coffee, freshly brewed
½ cup	Molasses
4 cups	Chicken Stock
½ cup	Water
3 Tbs	Cornstarch
	Salt

"Why would we include chicken livers in the Soby's cookbook? For one thing, they are great. For another, this recipe is a wonderful example of what we mean by New South Cuisine. Fried chicken livers have been a favorite of Southerners for ages and this preparation gives them a modern twist."

For the Onion Jam: Zest the orange and squeeze the juice into a saucepan. Add the remaining ingredients to the saucepan. Simmer on medium-low heat until most of liquid is gone and the sauce has thickened to a syrupy consistency, about 1 hour. The jam keeps up to one month covered in refrigerator.

For the Gravy: Cook the bacon stirring occasionally until it is crisp, but not burnt. Add the onions and cook until they are lightly caramelized (browned). Sprinkle the flour over the onions and bacon and stir so there are no lumps. Add the coffee, molasses, and chicken stock and simmer for 1 hour. As the sauce reduces, skim off any foam that comes to the top using a ladle or spoon. Whisk together the cornstarch and cold water to make a slurry. While the sauce is simmering, stir in the slurry and simmer for 5 more minutes. Taste the sauce and season with salt as needed. →

Livers:

	Vegetable Oil
1 lb	Chicken Livers
4 cups	Flour, divided
2 cups	Buttermilk
2	Eggs
2 Tbs	Black Pepper, coarsely ground
	Salt and Fresh Ground Black Pepper

Chef's Notebook

When you are reducing the jam, watch it carefully because it is more likely to burn as it thickens. Reduce the heat as the jam thickens to avoid scorching.

You can make the onion jam up to one month in advance and refrigerate it to use for many other recipes. We use it on mini-hamburgers (sliders), pork tenderloin, and biscuits to name a few.

For the Livers: Preheat the vegetable oil in a fryer or tall pot to 350°F. Remove any excess fat from the livers and separate the lobes. Rinse under cold running water and pat them dry with a paper towel. Whisk together the eggs and buttermilk to make an egg wash. Season half of the flour with the coarse ground pepper. Dust the livers with flour and tap off the excess. Place them, a few at a time, into the egg wash, and then coat them with the seasoned flour. Drop the livers in the oil in small batches and cook for approximately 2 to 3 minutes. Remove them from the oil and drain on a pan lined with paper towels. Season with salt and pepper.

Finish the Dish: Put some "red eye" gravy on a plate. Arrange three to five livers on the gravy. Serve with jam on the side.

Pairing Suggestion: Pinot Noir (Russian River). The meaty characteristic of many Russian River Pinots draws out the same characteristics from the bacon and liver flavors in this dish.

Soby's catering chef Mike Granata prepares to go for his third Guinness World Record at Fall for Greenville with 3,237 pounds of shrimp and grits; all proceeds went to Meals on Wheels and Loaves and Fishes
Photo by Tanya Ackerman

At the Fall for Greenville cooking school, fans watch as Soby's chef Rodney Freidank cooks up a dish on Saturday afternoon   Photo by Owen Riley Jr.

The Budweiser Clydesdales make their way down Main Street to kick off Fall for Greenville Friday afternoon
Photo by Owen Riley Jr.

Crowds packed Main Street on the opening night of Fall For Greenville
Photo by Alan DeVorsey

FALLING FOR GREENVILLE

DAVID: *"Fall for Greenville* will always have a special place in our hearts at Soby's. One reason is because we actually won The Silver Spoon Award for our food during the 1997 festival—before the restaurant was even open!"

CARL: "When we purchased the building in 1997, we were shooting for a September opening. We committed to *Fall for Greenville* early in the year. But September rolled around, the festival was getting close, and it was clear to us the restaurant was not going to be ready. So, the question became, 'Do we participate or not?' We wanted the exposure, but how, without a kitchen?"

DAVID: "So, we talked with Jason Ezell, the chef at Greenville Country Club at the time. He said, 'Use my kitchen. I'll order the food. You can do your prep for the festival after hours.' Then we talked with Bill and Judy Balsizer at Two Chefs Delicatessen on Main Street. They agreed that during the festival, we could store our product at Two Chefs—then take food from their location to our tent on the street. We couldn't have done *Fall for Greenville* our first year without help like this from friends, and an incredible effort from our staff."

RODNEY: "As the years passed, we continued to enlist help from our friends, families, and loyal customers to participate in this event. In my mind, the best thing about *Fall for Greenville* has always been what it does for the team spirit, of both staff and loyal guests. A big part of the fun for participating restaurants is the various competitions, including tent decorating, the waiter's race, bartender's mix-off, and of course, the food judging, including professional panels and the Peoples' Choice award. These competitions really bring a team together and remind us that we do this as much for fun as for a living. This kind of festival is something that makes Greenville unique! We're willing to close Main Street to throw a party."

Baked Oysters

Andouille Sausage, Collard Greens, Crawfish Tails, Creole Tomato Hollandaise

(Serves 6, 4 oysters each)

Oysters:

1 lb	Andouille Sausage, diced
	Olive Oil
2 cups	Yellow Onion, diced
2 Tbs	Soby's Creole Seasoning, see page 204
2 cups	Sweet and Sour Greens, see page 51, chopped
2 Tbs	Fresh Garlic, minced
1 lb	Crawfish Tail Meat, rough chopped
24	Large Oysters (Louisiana or Apalachicola)

Hollandaise:

¾ lb	Butter, melted
4	Egg Yolks
3 Tbs	White Wine
2 Tbs	Pernod
½ tsp	Shallot, minced
½ tsp	Fresh Garlic, minced
1 Tbs	Tomato Paste
1 tsp	Soby's Creole Seasoning, see page 204
1 tsp	Salt

"Oysters are very popular in the South. Here is our variation on the classic dish, Oysters Rockefeller. You can make the filling up to three days in advance and stuff the oysters right before serving."

For the Oysters: Sauté the andouille in a large skillet with a small amount of olive oil until it is somewhat crisp. Add the onion and sauté until soft. Add the creole seasoning, garlic, greens, and crawfish tails to the skillet and continue to cook for 5 to 10 minutes to marry the flavors. Set aside.

Open the oysters and leave them on the half shell. Remember to cut underneath the oysters to free them from their shell. Top each oyster with a generous mound of the filling.

For the Hollandaise: For detailed instructions on making the sauce, see "Hollandaise," at the end of this recipe.

Pour 1 inch of water into a saucepan and bring it to a boil. Place the yolks, wine, Pernod, shallot, and garlic in a mixing bowl. When the water boils, turn the heat to low. Place the bowl on top of the pan and whisk vigorously until the yolks become frothy, somewhat thick, and doubled in volume. Remove the yolks from the heat and slowly drizzle in the butter while whisking constantly. Add the tomato paste, creole seasoning, and salt just before serving.

Finish the Dish: Spoon some of the hollandaise on top of each filled oyster and place them under the broiler until they are lightly browned on top. Serve immediately.

Pairing Suggestion: An un-oaked Chardonnay (New World). Be sure the wine is not aged in oak barrels. Many Chardonnays now say "un-oaked" on the label. You want acidity in this wine, not the buttery mouthfeel of an oak-aged Chardonnay.

Hollandaise

Along with tomato, espagnole (brown sauce), velouté (a sauce made from white meat stock, like chicken), and béchamel (cream sauce), hollandaise is known as one of the great "mother sauces" in French cooking. The technique for hollandaise can be used to make a multitude of derivative sauces to complement many different flavor profiles.

To make two servings of hollandaise, you need 1 egg yolk, 1 teaspoon lemon juice, and 4 to 6 tablespoons butter, melted. Some recipes also call for a little shallot and white wine and I like to finish mine with a sprinkle of cayenne pepper.

Although hollandaise is actually a very simple sauce with simple ingredients, the first time you make it can be quite tricky. In fact, when we tested the recipe for the Baked Oysters topped with Creole Tomato Hollandaise, we were fortunate to have Abby Culin, our culinary intern, working on the recipe. As luck would have it, she had never made hollandaise. You guessed it. The sauce didn't turn out like it was supposed to, so we went back and did it again. This time with my coaching, Abby turned out a nice hollandaise. That night, she went home and wrote down what she learned. Here is her take on making hollandaise:

Abby Culin
Holding Stuffed Oysters

The most important thing about making hollandaise is to have everything ready before you start (the butter melted, water boiling, eggs and other ingredients in the bowl).

Before you put the bowl on the heat, whisk its contents together to break up the yolks. When you put the bowl over the water bath, turn the burner to low.

Whisk vigorously and be sure to keep the whisk low and in the mixture. The goal for this part of the method is to thicken the sauce without making scrambled eggs. If the yolks look like they are starting to harden, simply remove the bowl from the heat and keep whisking. Make sure to scrape the sides of the bowl with the whisk as you go, so all the mixture is getting beaten. When the mixture is smooth, return the bowl to the heat and continue whisking. Repeat this process as often as necessary until you can draw a line through the mixture with the whisk and it takes about a second to fill in. The eggs will have doubled in volume and be much lighter in color. Once you have reached that stage, take the bowl off of the heat.

Next, the melted butter must be added very slowly. The sauce can "break" (un-emulsify, or separate) if the butter is added too quickly. Place your bowl on a wet towel to steady it while you whisk. While whisking vigorously, drizzle in the melted butter very slowly. When you are done, the sauce should be thick, but not too thick to drop off a spoon and spread out gently. Season the hollandaise with a touch of cayenne pepper and a squirt of fresh lemon juice (or other ingredients as desired).

If the sauce breaks (looks like egg drop soup), do not throw it away. Put two egg yolks in a blender and blend until they are light yellow. While blending, slowly drizzle in the broken hollandaise until it is emulsified again.

1. Place eggs, wine, and shallots in a bowl.

2. Bring 1 inch of water to boil in a pot.

3. Whisk the eggs together.

4. Turn down the heat, place the bowl over the water, and whisk egg mixture.

5. Continue whisking as mixture thickens.

6. If the mix gets too hot, remove it from the heat for a minute.

7. When cooled, return to heat. Scrape the sides as you whisk.

8. The thickened mixture is ready to remove from heat and whisk in butter.

9. Place the bowl on a wet towel to steady.

10. Whisk quickly while drizzling butter slowly.

11. Perfect!

12. Not perfect (broken)! Try again!

Soups & Salads

76 • *Soby's She Crab Soup*

79 • *Watermelon Gazpacho*
Bay Scallop Ceviche, Corn Tortillas

80 • *Smoked Butternut Squash Soup*
Confit Chicken Leg, Chive Crème

84 • *Gumbo for Chef Paul*
Creole Mustard Fingerling Potato Salad

91 • *Romaine and Mustard Greens*
Garlic Herb Croutons, Baked Parmesan, Andouille Caesar Dressing

93 • *Baby Spinach Salad*
Dried Cranberries, Clemson Blue Cheese, Spiced Pecans,
Applewood Bacon Buttermilk Dressing, Shaved Smithfield Ham

94 • *Field Greens Salad with Dressings for All Seasons*
English Cucumbers, Grape Tomatoes, Tobacco Onions

Ginger Molasses Vinaigrette
Strawberry Poppy Seed Vinaigrette
Peach Rice Wine Vinaigrette
Applewood Bacon Pecan Vinaigrette

Soby's She Crab Soup

(Makes about 2 quarts of soup; serves 8)

Stock:

1½ lbs	Blue Crabs, broken in half
4 qts	Cold Water
½ cup	Yellow Onion, diced
¼ cup	Celery, diced
¼ cup	Carrot, peeled and diced
1 bulb	Garlic, cut in half
2	Bay Leaves
½ tsp	Dried Thyme
12	Black Peppercorns

Soup:

4 oz	Crab Roe*
2 pints	Heavy Cream
2 Tbs	Old Bay® Seasoning
1 cup	Dry Sherry
2 cups	Crab Stock
1 tsp	Worcestershire Sauce
4 Tbs	Cornstarch
1 lb	Lump Crabmeat
	Salt

*Order crab roe through *www.charlestonseafood.com*. It comes in 1-lb packages, so cut off what you need and freeze the rest tightly wrapped for up to three months.

"No food SCREAMS South Carolina quite like She Crab Soup. What originated in Scotland and came to the Carolinas in the 1700s as Partan Bree, a somewhat bland crab and rice soup, got its characteristic change in Charleston, South Carolina. In the mid-1800s William Deas, butler to Charleston mayor R. Goodwyn Rhett, decided to perk up the dish by adding crab roe (crab eggs) for a dinner in honor of President William Howard Taft. Hence the name, She Crab Soup. The crab roe may be hard to find, but don't let that stop you from making the soup. It is delicious with or without it...but don't skip the Sherry!"

For the Stock: Place all ingredients in a large stockpot and bring to a boil. As soon as the liquid starts to boil, reduce the heat and simmer for 1 hour. Occasionally skim off any foam that comes to the top. Strain the liquid through a fine sieve into a container. Discard all but the liquid. Chill the liquid and keep refrigerated or frozen until needed. The stock lasts about three days in the refrigerator.

For the Soup: Preheat the oven to 350°F. Spread the crab roe on a baking sheet and place it in the oven to dry. As the roe dries, remove the pan from the oven. Crumble the roe and mix it up several times to expose more roe to the heat. When all the roe is quite dry and crisp (it should take about 30 minutes total), use a coffee or spice grinder to grind it to a fine dust. Reserve the roe for garnishing the soup later.

Heat the heavy cream in a 4-quart saucepan. Meanwhile, in a bowl, whisk together the Old Bay Seasoning, Sherry, crab stock, Worcestershire sauce, and cornstarch. When the cream comes to a boil, vigorously whisk in the stock mixture. Allow the soup to simmer, stirring occasionally, for about 20 minutes. Carefully pick through the crabmeat and pull out any shells. Gently stir the crabmeat into the soup. Season with salt to taste.

Finish the Dish: Serve the soup hot, topped with a sprinkling of roe and a splash of Sherry.

Pairing Suggestion: Sherry (Spain). Sherry is the choice for this dish, because it is also a component in the recipe. Remember this principle for pairings of your own: if you use it in the dish, it will probably pair wonderfully! Various types of Sherry are available. Find a medium-dry Sherry, such as an Oloroso.

Watermelon Gazpacho
Bay Scallop Ceviche, Corn Tortillas
(Serves 6)

Soup:

1 tsp	Cumin Seeds
1 tsp	Coriander Seeds
4 cups	Watermelon, peeled, seeded, and cubed
½ cup	Seedless Cucumber, peeled and chopped
½ cup	Yellow Bell Pepper, chopped
½ cup	Red Onion, chopped
¼ cup	Cilantro Leaves
1	Lime, juiced
1 tsp	Salt
	Tortilla Chips

Ceviche:

1 lb	Bay Scallops
2 tsp	Jalapeño, seeded and finely diced
⅓ cup	Red Bell Pepper, diced
½ cup	Green Onion, thinly sliced
½ tsp	Fresh Garlic, minced
¼ cup	Cilantro Leaves
3	Limes, juiced
½ cup	Olive Oil
1 tsp	Salt

"You won't believe

how well this combination

works. A perfect balance

of sweetness, spiciness, and

acidity."

For the Soup: Place a small skillet on high heat. When the pan is quite warm, add the cumin and coriander seeds. Cook, stirring constantly until they are aromatic and begin to pop. Do not burn the spices! Grind the spices in a coffee or spice grinder until fine. Mix all the ingredients except the salt in a bowl. Purée in a blender in batches. Season with salt. Chill thoroughly. Gazpacho should be served very cold. Reserve tortilla chips for serving.

For the Ceviche: Remove the abductor muscles (the small muscle on the side of the scallop that opens and closes the shell). Work quickly with the scallops because they must remain very cold at all times. Combine all the ingredients in a bowl. Cover with plastic wrap and refrigerate at least 1 hour.

Finish the Dish: Arrange the ceviche in the center of a chilled soup bowl or martini glass and pour the cold gazpacho around it. Warm the tortilla chips and serve on the side.

Pairing Suggestion: Dry Chenin Blanc (Loire Valley, France). Because the soup is very cold, be sure the wine is at a classic white wine serving temperature, between 50-55°. Most of us drink whites too cold (at refrigerator temperature).

Smoked Butternut Squash Soup
Confit Chicken Leg, Chive Crème

(Makes about 2 quarts of soup, serves 8)

Chicken:

8	Chicken Leg Quarters
1 cup	Kosher Salt
⅓ cup	Brown Sugar
5 tsp	Granulated Garlic
25	Black Peppercorns, crushed
2 tsp	Ground White Pepper
½ tsp	Ground Cloves
1 tsp	Ground Ginger
1 tsp	Ground Nutmeg
3	Bay Leaves, crushed
2 tsp	Dry Thyme
2 qts	Chicken Stock

Soup:

4 cups	Butternut Squash, peeled, seeded, and cubed
	Hickory Wood Smoking Chips
1 Tbs	Olive Oil
½ cup	Yellow Onion, diced
1 qt	Chicken Stock
½ cup	Maple Syrup
2 Tbs	Cornstarch
1 pint	Heavy Cream
½ tsp	Cayenne Pepper
	Salt

"This is one of my favorite soups. The fall is my favorite time to cook and especially to eat. At the beginning of September—still undeniably summer in South Carolina—I start thinking (my wife might say dreaming) about butternut squash. The magic of this soup is the combination of smoky and salty butternut squash and the sweet maple syrup all held together in silky cream with just a kick of spice."

For the Chicken: Start at least one day ahead. Rinse the chicken legs and pat them dry. Make a dry spice mix with the remaining ingredients except the chicken stock. Generously coat the chicken pieces in the spice mix. Wrap the chicken legs in plastic wrap and refrigerate at least 24 hours and up to 3 days. Remove the plastic wrap from the chicken and rinse thoroughly under cold running water, rubbing the chicken with your hands to remove as much of the spice mix as possible. Heat the chicken stock in a pan large enough to hold the legs and the liquid. Bring to a boil. Reduce the heat and add the chicken legs. Simmer the chicken legs uncovered for about 1 hour or until they become quite tender. Remove the legs from the liquid and allow them to cool slightly. When the chicken is just cool enough to handle, remove the skin, pull the meat from the bones, and shred it with your hands. Use the chicken now or refrigerate until needed.

For the Soup: Smoke the butternut squash in a smoker or on the grill, for 3 to 5 minutes (see the method on page 49). The squash quickly picks up the smoke flavor and can become bitter if smoked too long.

Sauté the onion in a large soup pot with the olive oil until it is soft and lightly caramelized. Add the smoked butternut squash and the chicken stock. Bring to a boil. Reduce the heat and simmer uncovered for approximately 30 minutes or until the squash is very tender and falls apart when touched with a fork. Dissolve the cornstarch in the heavy cream, and then add it and the maple syrup to the soup. Bring to a simmer and cook for another 5 minutes. Purée in small batches in a blender. Season with cayenne pepper and salt to taste.

The soup can be made several days in advance and refrigerated until needed. Heat to serve. →

Chive Crème:

¼ lb	Fresh Chives
1 cup	Spinach Leaves
1 pint	Heavy Cream
	Salt

For the Chive Crème: Blanch the spinach and chives for 10 seconds and shock (see the method on page 131). Squeeze the spinach and chives to remove the excess water and finely chop. Place the chives and spinach in a blender with half the cream and purée until smooth. Remove the mixture from the blender and whisk in the remaining cream. Season to taste with the salt. Chill until needed.

Finish the Dish: Arrange a pile of warm chicken in the center of a heated soup bowl and pour the hot butternut soup around the chicken. Top with the chive crème.

Pairing Suggestion: Pinot Noir (Sonoma, Napa, Carneros).
The smokiness in an oak-aged Pinot is a perfect match for the smoke in the dish.

Gumbo for Chef Paul
Creole Mustard Fingerling Potato Salad

(Makes 1 gallon of soup and 1½ quarts of potato salad; serves 8 as entrées)

Gumbo:

1 lb	Chef Paul's Andouille Sausage*
¾ cup	Vegetable Oil
¾ cup	Flour
1 Tbs	Blackened Redfish Magic®*
½ cup	Green Bell Pepper, diced
½ cup	Yellow Bell Pepper, diced
½ cup	Red Bell Pepper, diced
½ cup	Celery, diced
½ cup	Vidalia® Onion, diced
½ cup	Green Onion, diced
¼ cup	Fresh Garlic, minced

1 cup	Roma Tomatoes, diced
2 cups	Okra, cut in ½-inch rounds
1 Tbs	Blackened Redfish Magic*
8 cups	Chicken Stock
¼ cup	Worcestershire Sauce
1 lb	Shrimp (21-25 ct), peeled and deveined
1 lb	Crawfish Tail Meat
	Salt

*Chef Paul's products can be purchased in many local supermarkets or at his Web site: *www.chefpaul.com.*

"**Why are we making** gumbo for Chef Paul? For one thing, because we had a 'once-in-a-lifetime' opportunity to work with the most warm, loving, and caring chef on the planet, not once, but twice! Two things about this gumbo are directly related to this great American Chef. The first is the very essence of the gumbo called the roux. Chef Paul taught me how to make the roux, as well as many other important culinary lessons, on his two visits. Second, when most people think of gumbo, they probably think of rice. Chef Paul grew up enjoying his with potato salad and he shared that wonderful combination with us on his most recent visit. So, enjoy Chef! We love you and miss you and hope to work with you again soon!"

For the Gumbo: Begin by cutting the andouille sausage into ½-inch cubes. Heat the oil in a large soup pot and add the andouille. Cook on medium heat for about 5 minutes until the andouille has given some of its flavor to the oil. Remove the sausage to a paper towel-lined plate and reserve for later use. Make the roux by whisking the flour into the hot oil (see "The Art of Roux," at the end of this recipe). Keep the heat on medium and stir constantly until the roux becomes dark brown. While you are cooking the roux, do not let the flour burn. The whole process should take about 20 to 30 minutes. When the roux is dark and nutty smelling, add the first tablespoon of Blackened Redfish Magic, peppers, celery, and onions. Cook on medium-low heat for about 10 minutes, stirring constantly. When the vegetables are tender, add the garlic, tomatoes, okra, and the second tablespoon of Blackened Redfish Magic. Cook for 5 minutes and then add the stock and the Worcestershire sauce. Simmer for about 20 minutes, then add the shrimp and crawfish. Cook for 5 minutes and taste for seasoning. Add more Blackened Redfish Magic and salt as needed. Keep warm to serve. →

Potato Salad:

2 lbs	Fingerling Potatoes, washed
½ cup	Vidalia® Onion, diced
½ cup	Celery, diced
¼ cup	Italian Parsley, chopped
2 Tbs	Creole Mustard
2 cups	Mayonnaise
	Salt and Fresh Ground Black Pepper

For the Potato Salad: Cut the fingerling potatoes into even bite-sized pieces. Place them in a pot with enough cold, salted water to cover and bring to a boil. Boil the potatoes for about 15 minutes or until they are fork tender. Drain the water from the potatoes and put them in a bowl big enough to hold all the ingredients. Add the rest of the ingredients and mix thoroughly but gently so you don't break up the potatoes. Season to taste with salt and pepper.

Finish the Dish: Place a large ladle of gumbo in a heated soup bowl. Place a scoop of potato salad in the middle of the bowl. Enjoy with hats off to Chef Paul!

Pairing Suggestion: India Pale Ale (IPA). The substance of a good IPA works well with the dark roux that serves as the basis of this recipe.

The Art of Roux

Roux (rooh) is the combination of flour and fat (oil), which is used primarily to thicken sauces and soups. In Cajun cuisine, roux is much more important than a mere thickener. It is also used as a flavor component. Gumbo and étouffée are two examples of dishes that can be made or broken by the quality of the roux preparation. A good cook should have a working understanding of how roux is made, how roux is used, and of how roux styles differ.

The first thing to remember is that roux must be cooked. If it is not cooked properly, the dish you use it in will taste and feel like flour. When roux is cooked out, the starchiness goes away. So, combine equal parts of flour and oil in a pan according to the quantity needed for a particular recipe. Then begin to cook on medium heat, stirring constantly.

It is very important to stir the roux constantly and to cover the entire bottom of the pan when stirring. If any part of the roux sits on the hot pan too long, it darkens and becomes bitter. And, if any part of the roux becomes bitter (burnt), it turns the entire roux bitter. For this reason, the less experience you have in making roux, the slower you should go.

As Chef Paul taught me, watch the smoke coming from the pan while you work. If the smoke is white or light colored, you are doing great. If the smoke starts to turn dark, the pan is too hot and you are in danger of burning the roux. Remove the pan from the heat and continue whisking until the smoke lightens again.

After about 5 minutes, the roux should smell a bit like popcorn and have darkened slightly. This stage is called pale roux, which is normally used for thickening cream sauces and other light-colored sauces and soups. At this stage the roux has its greatest thickening power. As roux cooks longer, it becomes darker and has less thickening power, but the flavor grows more intense. Keep stirring the roux until the color is right for the dish you are creating. The photos show the different stages of roux.

When you use roux to thicken soups and sauces, simmer them for at least 20 minutes after adding the roux to maximize the roux's thickening power and cook out the starch.

1.Mix the flour and oil.

2. Pale Roux.
Keep Whisking.

3. Brown Roux.
Keep Whisking.

4. Dark Brown Roux.
Done!

SERVING OTHERS

For Soby's, hospitality is not just about making guests feel good by offering a smile, providing some good food, and pouring them a cold drink after a hard day.

Hospitality is also about serving others in a more profound way. One of our guiding philosophies is that if we take care of others, they will take care of us. That has proven true time and time again.

We also believe a community succeeds only when all its residents play an active role in building and maintaining it. One way we try to play such a role is by using our talents and time to raise money for those less fortunate than us. Over the years, we have hosted golf tournaments to raise money for organizations including Make-a-Wish Foundation;

Loaves and Fishes, a local organization supplying surplus food items to soup kitchens and food banks; and Greenville Family Partnership, which helps keep children off drugs.

In addition, each year we celebrate the founding of Soby's with a fundraising event, during which we announce the three major organizations we will support during the coming year. These groups generally fall into categories about which our staff cares deeply: food related—feeding the hungry in our area; caring for children—supporting mistreated children or educating them to build a better future; and medical—donating to a charity such as the Susan G. Komen Breast Cancer Foundation, as requested by one or more of our staff members.

Some of our best life experiences have also come from the events we've held to generate funds to help others. One of those was the opportunity to work with Chefs Paul Prudhomme and Keith Keogh in 1999, who came to Greenville for a charity dinner in support of a local children's shelter.

CARL: "The dinner was made possible by a great friend and mentor, who was taken from us senselessly and unexpectedly. I don't know if I would be where I am today, if I hadn't met and learned so much from Jim Cockman. Jim was responsible for putting on a dinner for Pendleton Place Children's Shelter. It was held Valentine's Day, 1999. I remember being very intimidated by Chef Paul and Chef Keith Keogh before meeting them. All of us wondered if they would approve of what we were doing at Soby's. This dinner, less than eighteen months after opening, was a huge event for us—to have two such prominent figures in the culinary world working in our kitchen, demonstrating their passion to our team; serving as examples of where our passion could take us."

Chef Rodney Freidank, Ryan Freidank, and Chef Paul Prudhomme

Southern Exposure Taste of the South, Friday evening informal dinner by the Reedy River   Photo by Douglas Smith

RODNEY: "I was nervous as well. I remember working on an hors d'oeuvre for the dinner, when Chef Paul came over and asked me what I was making. I fumbled through some answer about the dish being loosely based on the classic dish Cassoulet, but not knowing what I would call it. He tasted it and replied, 'I know what I would call it... delicious.' Imagine how I felt then! I wasn't intimidated after that. I just wanted to listen and learn all I could from both of those great chefs."

Soby's team members also serve on the boards of many charitable organizations, including The American Red Cross, The March of Dimes, Share our Strength, and Dogs for Disabled.

Community service has even become an "official" part of what we do as a company. In 2006, Carl Sobocinski joined forces with Greenville native and platinum recording artist, Edwin McCain, to form Local Boys Do Good—a non-profit foundation created to make an even greater impact by combining their fundraising efforts.

The product of Carl's and Edwin's efforts is *Southern Exposure*. This three-day food, wine, and music festival is held every September in Greenville, SC. The event showcases national culinary talent such as Thomas Keller (The French Laundry, Yountville, CA); Bob Kinkead (Kinkead's, Washington DC); and Gerry Klaskala (Aria, Atlanta), and Frank Lee (Slightly North of Broad, Charleston). In addition, Master Sommeliers Bob Bath, Laura Williamson, and Wayne Belding have participated. Add entertainment—including five-time Grammy winner Michael McDonald, three-time Grammy winner Branford Marsalis, and Greenville's own Edwin McCain—and there is a good chance our two "local boys" and the Soby's team have only begun to show what serving others really means.

Romaine and Mustard Greens
Garlic Herb Croutons, Baked Parmesan, Andouille Caesar Dressing

(Makes about 1 pint of dressing; serves 6 to 8)

Salad Greens*:

2 heads	Romaine Lettuce, washed and cut into bite-sized pieces
½ lb	Mustard Greens, washed and cut into bite-sized pieces

*Figure a ratio of 2 to 1, romaine to mustard greens, for this salad.

Dressing:

¼ cup	Andouille Sausage, diced
1 Tbs	Olive Oil
1	Egg Yolk
2 Tbs	Red Wine Vinegar
2 Tbs	Balsamic Vinegar
2 Tbs	Lemon Juice, freshly squeezed
1 tsp	Fresh Garlic, minced
1½ tsp	Fresh Ground Black Pepper
1 Tbs	Worcestershire Sauce
1 cup	Olive Oil
½ cup	Parmesan Cheese, grated

Croutons:

4 cups	Rustic Bread, cut into ½-inch cubes (preferably day-old bread)
	Olive Oil
¼ cup	Italian Parsley, finely chopped
1 Tbs	Granulated Garlic
1 Tbs	Granulated Onion
	Salt

Baked Parmesan:

2 cups	Parmesan Cheese, finely shredded

> *"Caesar Salad remains popular in restaurants everywhere. Here is a New South version you will love. My favorite way to make croutons is to fry them, but you can bake them if you like."*

For the Dressing: Cook the andouille sausage in olive oil until crisp. Drain on paper towels and reserve. With an immersion blender, purée the yolks, vinegars, lemon juice, garlic, pepper, and Worcestershire sauce in a mixing bowl. Add the andouille and slowly drizzle in the 1 cup oil, while continuing to blend. Add the Parmesan cheese and season with salt as needed. Refrigerate until ready to use.

For the Croutons: Fry the bread cubes in a small amount of olive oil until they are crisp. Place the croutons in a bowl and toss with the parsley, garlic, and onion. Season to taste with salt.

For the Baked Parmesan: Preheat the oven to 350°F. Place a sheet of wax paper on a baking sheet and spray with cooking spray. Sprinkle some of the Parmesan on the paper to form a 3-inch diameter circle. Repeat until the pan is full. Bake about 10 minutes until the Parmesan is crisp and lightly browned. Cool before serving to ensure the cheese is completely crisp.

Finish the Dish: Toss the salad greens and croutons with the dressing. Place a mound of the greens and croutons in the center of a salad plate or bowl and top with a Parmesan crisp.

Pairing Suggestion: Vernaccia or Verdicchio (Italy). Either of these Italian white wines is a refreshing complement to the andouille and the saltiness of the dressing.

Baby Spinach Salad

Dried Cranberries, Clemson Blue Cheese, Spiced Pecans, Applewood Bacon Buttermilk Dressing, Shaved Smithfield Ham

(Makes about 1 pint of dressing and lots of pecans for snacking; serves 6 to 8)

Dressing:

½ lb	Applewood Smoked Bacon, diced
1 cup	Buttermilk
1 cup	Mayonnaise
1 Tbs	Prepared Horseradish
½ tsp	Fresh Garlic, minced
1½ tsp	Lemon Juice, freshly squeezed
1½ tsp	Granulated Garlic
1½ tsp	Granulated Onion
¼ tsp	Cayenne Pepper
2 Tbs	Italian Parsley, chopped
1½ tsp	Fresh Basil, chopped
1½ tsp	Fresh Chives, chopped
1½ Tbs	Fresh Dill Fronds, chopped

Spiced Pecans:

1 lb	Pecan Halves
½ cup	Sugar
1 Tbs	Soby's Creole Seasoning, see page 204
1	Egg White, whisked until frothy

Salad:

6 cups	Baby Spinach, washed and dried
1 cup	Spiced Pecans
½ cup	Dried Cranberries
½ cup	Clemson Blue Cheese, crumbled
6 slices	Smithfield Ham,* shaved

*Substitute prosciutto if Smithfield ham is not available.

"Mike Goot, one of our best customers and friends, told me he would never come to Soby's again if we didn't put this salad right back on the menu. So, of course, we did! We don't usually respond to that kind of blackmail (okay, we actually enjoy it), but this dish really is a great combination of flavors and textures."

For the Dressing: Cook the bacon in a skillet until it is crisp and has rendered all its fat. Pour the bacon and fat into a bowl. Add the rest of the ingredients and blend together using an immersion blender or a whisk, if you prefer the dressing a bit chunky. Serve chilled. Store any unused dressing in the refrigerator.

For the Spiced Pecans: Preheat the oven to 350°F. Spray a baking sheet with cooking spray. Mix all ingredients together and spread on the baking sheet. Bake, stirring every 5 minutes until the nuts look dry. Remove the pecans from the oven and allow them to cool. The nuts will not be crisp until they are completely cool.

Finish the Dish: Toss the baby spinach, 1 cup spiced pecans, the cranberries, and cheese with a scoop of dressing in a bowl. Mound dressed spinach on a salad plate and top with the shaved ham or prosciutto.

Pairing Suggestion: Chardonnay (New or Old World). The buttermilk dressing and texture of the Chardonnay work well together. Choose one of your favorites.

Field Greens Salad with Dressings for All Seasons

English Cucumbers, Grape Tomatoes, Tobacco Onions

(Makes about 1 pint of each salad dressing; salad serves 6 to 8)

Salad:

6-8 cups	Salad Greens, washed and cut into bite-sized pieces
1	English Cucumber, peeled if desired and sliced
1 pint	Grape Tomatoes (or any tomato in season)

Tobacco Onions:

1	Yellow Onion (jumbo), thinly sliced
	Vegetable Oil
	Salt

"One thing that is always on the menu is a simple mixed greens salad. What changes the most about the salad over time is the dressing, as we try to use seasonal ingredients. In this recipe, I have chosen ingredients that seem to do well year round for the main part of the salad. You can use your choice of greens. Hydroponically grown cucumbers are perfect all year long and grape tomatoes seem to be the best tomato you can get in the middle of the winter (although I would strongly encourage you to buy any locally grown tomato that is picked completely ripe). The nice sweet flavor and delicate crunch of the tobacco onions provide a textural contrast to your standard spring mix lettuces. Store any unused dressings in the refrigerator."

For the Tobacco Onions: Heat the oil in a fryer or a deep pot to 350°F. Loosely drop the onions, in small batches, into the oil. Use a spoon or a skimmer to gently move the onions around while they are cooking so that they do not stick together and they cook evenly. Do not let them get too dark or they turn bitter. When the onions just start to turn golden brown, remove them from the hot oil and spread on a paper towel-lined baking sheet. The onions continue to darken after being removed from the fryer until they cool enough to stop cooking. Using a pair of tongs, lift up some of the onions at a time and separate them, allowing them to dry as they cool. Season with salt.

Finish the Dish: Toss the greens with one of the seasonal dressings on the following pages and pile high on a salad plate. Garnish with the cucumbers and tomatoes and top with a loose nest of the tobacco onions.

Pairing Suggestion: Sauvignon Blanc (New Zealand). A Marlborough or Martinborough Sauvignon Blanc has the acidity and minerality to stand up to these vinaigrette dressings. →

Ginger Molasses Vinaigrette (Winter):

½ cup	Orange Juice
¼ cup	Molasses
1 Tbs	Pickled Ginger
½ tsp	Fresh Garlic, minced
1 Tbs	Dijon Mustard
1 Tbs	Soy Sauce
1 tsp	Sesame Oil
1 Tbs	Black Sesame Seeds
1¼ cups	Canola Oil

For the Winter Vinaigrette: Place all ingredients except the oils and the sesame seeds in a blender. Blend on high and drizzle in the sesame oil and the vegetable oil. Stir in the sesame seeds.

∞∞∞

Strawberry Poppy Seed Vinaigrette (Spring):

2 Tbs	Red Onion, chopped
¼ cup	Sugar
2 Tbs	White Balsamic Vinegar
1 cup	Strawberries, stems removed
1 Tbs	Poppy Seeds
1½ cups	Canola Oil

For the Spring Vinaigrette: Place all ingredients except the oil and salt in a blender. Purée until smooth. While blending, drizzle in the oil until dressing is emulsified.

Peach Rice Wine Vinaigrette (Summer):

2	Shallots, peeled
1 tsp	Olive Oil
½ cup	Ripe Peaches, peeled and cut into chunks
1 tsp	Pickled Ginger
¼ cup	Rice Wine Vinegar
¼ cup	Sugar
2 tsp	Soy Sauce
1 cup	Canola Oil

For the Summer Vinaigrette: Preheat the oven to 350°F. Coat the shallots in the olive oil and wrap them in aluminum foil. Roast them for approximately 40 minutes or until they become tender and caramelized. Place all ingredients except the oil in a blender. Blend until smooth. While blending, drizzle in the oil until dressing is emulsified.

∞∞∞

Applewood Bacon Pecan Vinaigrette (Fall):

¼ cup	Applewood Smoked Bacon, diced small
1 cup	Pecan Vinegar
½ cup	Dark Brown Sugar
1 Tbs	Dijon Mustard
1 cup	Canola Oil

For the Fall Vinaigrette: Place the bacon in a hot skillet and cook until crisp. Add the vinegar to the pan and stir to remove any bacon stuck to the bottom of the pan. Add the brown sugar and stir until it is dissolved. Add the mustard and drizzle in the oil while whisking vigorously. Remove from the stove and cool.

Small Plates

101 • *Grillades and Grits*
Hickory Smoked Beef Tenderloin, Exotic Mushrooms, Roasted Garlic,
Creamy White Cheddar Grits

103 • *Lowcountry Shrimp*
Watauga County Ham, Kiwifruit, Chardonnay Cream

104 • *Sautéed Soft Shell Crab*
Asparagus Potato Hash, Lemon Tarragon Butter

109 • *Braised Duck Leg with Chipotle BBQ*
Spicy Cabbage Slaw, Sweet Potato Biscuit

113 • *Caramelized St. Louis Pork Ribs*
Truffled Potato Salad, Crispy Vidalia® Onions,
Mustard BBQ Sauce

117 • *Sweet Potato Gnocchi*
Applewood Smoked Bacon, Wilted Spinach,
Toasted Pecans, Sage Brown Butter Sauce

121 • *Lobster Cobbler*
Summer Vegetables, Coconut Curry Sauce,
Savory Lime Crumb Topping

123 • *Seared Foie Gras*
Old Poinsett Hotel Spoonbread,
Caramelized Pineapple Butter Sauce

Grillades and Grits
Hickory Smoked Beef Tenderloin, Exotic Mushrooms, Roasted Garlic, Creamy White Cheddar Grits

(Serves 6)

Grillades:

2 lbs	Beef Tenderloin Chunks
	Hickory Smoking Chips
2 Tbs	Olive Oil
1 lb	Exotic Mushrooms (Cremini, Shiitake, Portobello)
2 cups	Yellow Onion, cut into large strips
2 Tbs	Fresh Garlic, minced
¼ cup	Vegetable Oil
¼ cup	Flour
3 cups	Beef Stock
¼ cup	Roasted Garlic Cloves, whole, see page 208
2 Tbs	Worcestershire Sauce
1 Tbs	Texas Pete® Hot Sauce
1 pint	Heavy Cream
	Salt and Fresh Ground Black Pepper

Grits:

4 cups	Chicken Stock
2 tsp	Salt
1 cup	Stone Ground White Grits
¼ cup	Red Bell Pepper, diced
¼ cup	Green Bell Pepper, diced
½ cup	Red Onion, diced
½ cup	Heavy Cream
1 cup	White Cheddar Cheese, shredded
	Salt and Fresh Ground Black Pepper

"I still remember when we first added this dish to the menu at Soby's. In New Orleans, Claudia and I had eaten at a bunch of great restaurants (as any self-respecting chef would do on his honeymoon) and learned what a grillade (gree-YAHD) was—a piece of steak that is pounded, seared in hot fat, and braised until tender. Soby's creamy white cheddar grits were already the talk of the town back at home and I was easily inspired to create our own version of the classic New Orleans' favorite."

For the Grillades: Start by smoking the beef with the hickory chips, for approximately 5 minutes (see the method on page 49). Sauté the mushrooms in olive oil on high heat in small batches. Remove the mushrooms from the pan and set them aside. Add the onions to the pan and cook until soft and caramelized. Add the fresh minced garlic and cook 2 minutes, until the garlic releases its flavor. Do not brown the garlic. Add the vegetable oil and stir in the flour to make a roux. Cook for 4 to 6 minutes, stirring constantly to prevent the roux from burning. Add 1 cup of the beef stock and bring it to a simmer, stirring to prevent lumps. Stir in the rest of the beef stock and the remaining ingredients. Cook for about 20 minutes to reduce the sauce and cook the starchiness out of the roux. Add the beef and mushrooms and bring to a simmer. Simmer for 5 minutes. Season to taste with salt and pepper.

For the Grits: Combine the stock and salt in a saucepan over medium-high heat. When the stock comes to a boil, whisk in the grits until smooth. Reduce the heat to low and simmer for approximately 20 minutes, stirring often to prevent the grits from sticking to the bottom of the pan. Add the peppers and onions and cook for another 5 minutes. Stir in the cream and the cheddar cheese. Season to taste with salt and pepper.

Finish the Dish: Serve the grillades over the white cheddar grits. If desired, top with two fried quail eggs or a fried chicken egg and garnish with diced tomatoes and green onions.

Pairing Suggestion: Rhône-style red (New or Old World). The smoked-meat overtones of many Grenache-Syrah blends match this dish perfectly.

Lowcountry Shrimp
Watauga County Ham, Kiwifruit, Chardonnay Cream

(Serves 6)

Shrimp:

½ lb	Country Ham,* sliced ⅛ inch thick
1 Tbs	Olive Oil
1 tsp	Crushed Red Pepper Flakes
2 lbs	Shrimp (21–25 ct),* peeled and deveined
1½ cups	Chardonnay
6	Kiwifruit, peeled and diced
1 pint	Heavy Cream
1 tsp	Cornstarch
1 Tbs	Water
	Salt and Fresh Ground Black Pepper

*For sources of ham and shrimp, see the New South Pantry.

"Here is an award-winning dish that uses two great Carolina ingredients: Port Royal Shrimp and Watauga County Country Ham. Your guests will be surprised at how well balanced the unusual flavor combination is."

For the Shrimp: Dice the ham. Heat the olive oil in a large skillet. Add the ham and red pepper flakes. Sauté until the ham becomes slightly crisp and has given its flavor to the oil. Add the shrimp and sauté until the shrimp are half cooked, about 2 minutes. Remove the shrimp and reserve. Add the wine to the pan and simmer to reduce by half. Add the kiwifruit and the heavy cream and simmer until the liquid is reduced by half again. Add the shrimp and cook until the shrimp are completely cooked, about 2 more minutes. Mix together the cornstarch and water to make a slurry. With the sauce boiling, drizzle in the slurry until the sauce becomes thick enough to coat the back of a spoon. Season to taste with salt and pepper.

Finish the Dish: Serve with crusty French bread or jalapeño cornbread and garnish with fresh diced kiwifruit.

Pairing Suggestion: Chardonnay (Russian River). You can use a "big" Chardonnay with this dish to enhance the wine used in the cream sauce.

Sautéed Soft Shell Crab

Asparagus Potato Hash, Lemon Tarragon Butter

(Serves 6)

Hash:

½ lb	Asparagus
1½ lbs	Idaho Potatoes
1½ lbs	Sweet Potatoes
2 cups	Vidalia® Onions, diced
2 Tbs	Olive Oil
2 Tbs	Butter
2 Tbs	Italian Parsley, finely chopped
	Salt and Fresh Ground Black Pepper

Butter Sauce:

1 cup	White Wine
1	Lemon, juiced
½ tsp	Fresh Garlic, minced
2 Tbs	Fresh Tarragon Leaves, chopped
½ lb	Unsalted Butter
	Salt and Fresh Ground Black Pepper

"I created this recipe for my mom. One of the local television stations had asked me to do a cooking segment the week before Mother's Day. As luck would have it, that is prime soft shell crab season and beautiful South Carolina asparagus is also available. So I invited Mom to come with me and made two of her favorite things. We served this dish topped with an egg for Mother's Day Brunch. You can eat it whenever you are in the mood, with or without the egg. Mom, this one's for you."

For the Hash: Pick up each piece of asparagus with the thumb and forefinger of both hands holding one hand near the tip and the other at the base. Gently bend the asparagus until it breaks. Discard the base piece or save it to make asparagus soup. If the asparagus is thicker than a pencil, peel it from just below the tip to the base to remove the tough skin. Blanch the asparagus for 30 seconds and shock (see the method on page 131). When the asparagus is cold, slice it into ¼-inch pieces, leaving the tips in tact.

Peel the potatoes and cut into ¼-inch dice. Keep the Idaho potatoes in water until ready to use, so they do not turn brown. Sauté the onions in the olive oil, until tender and lightly caramelized. Add the potatoes and cook until they are fork tender and caramelized. Add the asparagus and the butter and heat through. Add the parsley. Season to taste with salt and pepper.

For the Butter Sauce: Put the wine, tarragon, garlic, and lemon juice in a saucepan and bring to a boil. Reduce the heat and simmer until the liquid is reduced by three-quarters. Remove the sauce from the heat and quickly whisk in the butter. Season to taste with salt and pepper. →

Crabs:

6	Soft Shell Crabs, trimmed
2 tsp	Soby's Creole Seasoning, see page 204
2 tsp	Salt
2 cups	Flour
	Olive Oil

For the Crabs: Dust the crabs with the creole seasoning and salt. Dredge the crabs in the flour and shake off any excess. Heat olive oil in a skillet over medium-high heat. Sauté two or three crabs at a time until crisp, about 2 minutes. Do not overcrowd the pan. Flip the crabs and sauté the other side for 2 more minutes. Keep warm until all are cooked.

Finish the Dish: Arrange some of the potato hash in the center of a plate. Place a crab on top of the hash. Spoon some of the butter sauce over the crab. Serve with crusty bread to soak up the extra sauce. If desired, serve with a sunnyside-up egg on top.

Pairing Suggestion: Sauvignon Blanc (Napa, Sonoma, Mendocino). The crispness of the Sauvignon Blanc works well with the richness of the crab.

Chef's Notebook

Have your fishmonger trim the crabs for you, or do it yourself:

1. Lift up the top shell on both sides and trim out the gills with kitchen shears.

2. Snip across the shell below the eyes.

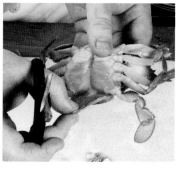

3. Lift up the triangle-shaped piece (the apron) on the underside and remove it.

Braised Duck Leg with Chipotle BBQ
Spicy Cabbage Slaw, Sweet Potato Biscuit

(Serves 6)

Duck Leg:

6	Duck Legs
½ cup	Texas Pete® Hot Sauce
½ lb	Brown Sugar
2 Tbs	Salt

Barbecue Sauce: (yields 3–4 cups)

1 cup	Vidalia® Onion, diced
	Olive Oil
1 tsp	Fresh Garlic, minced
2 cups	Apple Cider Vinegar
⅔ cup	Ketchup
1 cup	Brown Sugar, packed
½ cup	Molasses
1 Tbs	Worcestershire Sauce
2	Chipotle Peppers, (canned in Adobo)
1 tsp	Ground Ginger
½ tsp	Cumin Seed

Slaw:

½ cup	Red Onion, diced
1	Jalapeño, seeded and finely diced
½ cup	Cilantro Leaves
2	Limes, juiced
½ cup	Red Wine Vinegar
2 cups	Mayonnaise
4 cups	Green Cabbage, shredded
1 cup	Red Cabbage, shredded
½ cup	Carrot, peeled and shredded
½ cup	Cilantro Leaves, rough chopped
	Salt and Fresh Ground Black Pepper

"This dish is as delicious as it is beautiful. You can adjust the spiciness to your liking, but don't be fooled by the spice level in the sauce before it is caramelized on the duck leg. The caramelization sweetens the sauce, balancing the spice."

For the Duck Leg: Place the legs, hot sauce, sugar, and salt in a pot large enough to hold all the ingredients. Add water to cover and bring to a boil. Reduce heat to a simmer. Simmer for 1½ to 2 hours or until the duck is tender. While the duck legs are cooking, prepare the barbeque sauce. Remove the duck legs from the water and let them cool. Once the legs are cool, carefully remove the thighbone by gently twisting it and pulling it from the meat. Removing the bone is optional, but it makes for a nicer presentation and easier eating.

Heat a charcoal or gas grill to medium, medium-high heat. Put the duck legs on the grill and baste with the barbecue sauce until caramelized. Be careful not to burn the sauce.

For the Barbecue Sauce: Sauté the onion in olive oil until light brown. Add the garlic and sauté for 2 minutes being careful not to burn the garlic. Add the remaining ingredients. Simmer for 40 minutes on low heat stirring often. Purée the mixture in a blender. Chill until ready to use.

For the Slaw: Begin by making the dressing. Place the onion, jalapeño, whole cilantro leaves, and lime juice in a food processor and purée to a paste. Add the vinegar and mayonnaise and process to combine. Season the dressing to taste with salt and pepper. Place the remaining ingredients in a bowl and toss with enough dressing to achieve the desired level of creaminess. Refrigerate the slaw and remaining dressing. →

Biscuits:

1	Sweet Potato (large)
1¾ cups	Flour
3 tsp	Baking Powder
2 tsp	Brown Sugar
1 tsp	Table Salt
2 Tbs	Shortening
	Additional flour for countertop (bench flour)
¼ cup	Buttermilk
2 Tbs	Butter, melted

For the Biscuits: Preheat the oven to 375°F. Bake the sweet potato for about 30 to 40 minutes, until fork tender. Peel the sweet potato and push it through a food mill or ricer. Sift together the flour, baking powder, and salt. Put the dry ingredients and sugar in the bowl of a food processor. Add ¾ cup of the sweet potato and all of the shortening. Pulse until the mixture is crumbly. With the processor running, drizzle in the buttermilk until the mixture forms a sticky ball.

Pour the dough onto a work surface that has been liberally dusted with flour. Press or roll the dough to ½-inch thickness. Cut the dough into 3-inch diameter rounds and space evenly on a greased baking sheet. Bake for 10 to 15 minutes until the biscuits become golden on top and cooked in the middle. Brush the biscuits with melted butter after removing from the oven. Serve warm.

Finish the Dish: Cut the top off a biscuit and place the bottom half in the center of a plate. Place a bit of the slaw on top of the biscuit. Put the barbequed duck leg on top of the slaw. Garnish with extra barbeque sauce and the biscuit top if you like.

Pairing Suggestions: Pilsner-style beer or Zinfandel (Sonoma). Barbeque is always great with beer. To make the meal more elegant, serve a jammy Zinfandel to complement the duck. Ask your retailer for something from the Alexander Valley for a special treat.

Chef's Notebook

Although this recipe has several components, you can make many of them ahead of time. Make the slaw dressing up to one week ahead and refrigerate. Mix the slaw up to 12 hours ahead and refrigerate. Cook and cool the duck legs up to three days ahead and finish them on the grill on the day you serve the dish. Make the barbeque sauce up to one month ahead and refrigerate. For the biscuits, bake the sweet potato a day ahead and keep refrigerated. Make the biscuits the day you serve this dish.

To save money, buy whole ducks and remove the leg quarters (as you would on a chicken) to use in this recipe. Slice the breast halves off the bone by running your knife under the breast along the bone until they are free. Sear the duck breasts skin side down in a hot skillet until the skin is crisp and then use the same barbeque sauce to finish the breasts on the grill. Cook to medium-rare or medium to keep them tender.

Riders set a fast pace in the first lap of the 2006 USA Cycling Pro Championships in Greenville
Photo by Patrick Collard

TOUR DE GREENVILLE

Every July, cycling fans at Soby's and around the world crowd around their televisions to check the latest standings in the Tour de France. Greenville has had an even keener interest than most American cities, because Greenville's own George Hincapie played a key role on the U.S. Postal and Discovery teams that rode Lance Armstrong to his record-breaking seven Tour victories. George claimed his first individual stage win with a stunning ride in the mountains at Pla d'Adet during the 2005 Tour.

Since September 2006, however, Greenville residents have been able just to step out Soby's front doors and see world-class cycling! After two decades in Philadelphia (during which race winners included Eric Heiden, Greg LeMond, and Lance Armstrong), the Cycling Professional Championships have moved to downtown Greenville, SC. George Hincapie won the 2006 Road Race Championships before a cheering crowd of 62,000 along the course, finishing just a block away from Soby's Court Square location. David Zabriskie, of Salt Lake City, UT, won the Individual Time Trial Championship over a scenic course in the rolling hills adjacent to The Cliffs Communities.

With the Greenville Hospital System serving as title sponsor for the event, and The Cliffs presenting the Professional Time Trial Championship, Greenville's enthusiastic support of professional cycling is clear. Hincapie™ Sportswear, created by George's brother Rich Hincapie to meet the need for quality cycling apparel worldwide, is also located in Greenville. And in 2007, it was announced that George, Rich, and PHC Communities would launch Pla d'Adet, a unique cycling resort and training community near the Blue Ridge Mountains just north of Greenville.

Above: George Hincapie takes the lead during the 2006 USA Cycling Pro Championships in Greenville

George Hincapie celebrates with his wife Melanie after winning the 2006 USA Cycling Pro Championships in Greenville

Photos by Patrick Collard

Caramelized St. Louis Pork Ribs

Truffled Potato Salad, Crispy Vidalia® Onions, Mustard BBQ Sauce

(Serves 6, with plenty of potato salad)

Ribs:

3 racks	St. Louis Style Pork Ribs (½ rack per person)
½ cup	Texas Pete® Hot Sauce
1 cup	Brown Sugar, packed
2 Tbs	Salt
	Water to cover

Barbecue Sauce:

2 cups	Cattlemen's® Southern Gold Barbecue Sauce
¼ cup	Worcestershire Sauce
2 Tbs	Prepared Horseradish
2 Tbs	Texas Pete Hot Sauce

"Chef Shane White shared this family recipe for the barbeque sauce with us when he was a sous chef at Soby's. We won a Silver Spoon award with this dish because the flavors are so amazing together. I know it may be a little difficult to get the truffle oil, but please do. It is what sets this potato salad apart from all the rest. We would normally make the barbeque sauce from scratch, but Shane's family uses Cattlemen's Southern Gold Barbecue sauce as a base. It is so good that we made the exception. You should too!"

For the Ribs: Place the whole rib racks in a roasting pan or saucepot (cut the racks in half if they don't fit in your pan). Cover them with the rest of the ingredients and top with aluminum foil. Cook the ribs in a 350°F oven for about 2 hours or until they are tender enough to just about fall off the bone. Remove the pan from the oven and uncover it. Allow the ribs to sit until they are cool enough to handle, but not more than 30 minutes. Carefully remove the racks from the liquid and place flat on a platter or baking sheet. Refrigerate to cool completely, 1 hour to overnight. Meanwhile, make the barbeque sauce.

Heat the grill to medium. Cut the ribs into double-cut portions (two bones per piece). Baste the ribs with the barbeque sauce and place on the grill. Heat until the ribs are hot, basting every 5 minutes or so. Take care not to burn the sauce.

For the Barbecue Sauce: Whisk together all ingredients. Refrigerate until needed. →

Potato Salad:

4 lbs	Idaho Potatoes
½ cup	Celery, diced
½ cup	Yellow Onion, diced
2 cups	Mayonnaise
1 bunch	Italian Parsley, chopped
1 Tbs	White Truffle-Infused Olive Oil*
	Salt and Fresh Ground Black Pepper

*Available at *www.culinaryneeds.com*

Onions:

	Vegetable Oil
1	Vidalia® Onion, thinly sliced
4 cups	Flour
2	Eggs
1 cup	Buttermilk
2 Tbs	Soby's Creole Seasoning, see page 204
	Salt and Fresh Ground Black Pepper

For the Potato Salad: Peel the potatoes and cut into medium dice (so you can fit two pieces on a teaspoon). Try to make the potatoes all the same size, so they cook in the same amount of time. Put the potatoes in a saucepan and cover with lightly salted cold water. Bring the water to a boil over high heat. Reduce the heat so the boiling continues, but the water does not boil over. Cook until tender, about 10 to 15 minutes. Drain the potatoes. Mix all ingredients in a bowl and toss them by hand so the potatoes do not break up too much. Season to taste with salt and pepper. Refrigerate until ready to serve.

For the Onions: Preheat the oil in a fryer or large pot to 350°F degrees. Separate the onion rings and put them in a container with 1 cup of the flour. Mix the eggs and the buttermilk. Shake off the excess flour and transfer the rings into the egg mixture. Once the rings are coated well, transfer them into a bowl with the rest of the flour. Gently shake off the excess flour once again and drop them into the hot oil. Stir gently to prevent clumping. When they are golden brown and crisp, about 2 to 3 minutes, remove the rings and drain on a paper towel-lined pan. Add salt and pepper to taste. Serve immediately.

Finish the Dish: Place a spoonful of the potato salad in the middle of a plate. Cross stack the ribs on top of the potato salad. Build a nest of onions on top of the ribs. Serve with plenty of paper towels!

Pairing Suggestion: Pinot Noir (Willamette Valley). The characteristics of a nice Oregon Pinot make this wine a great match to bring out the flavor of the truffles in the potato salad.

Chef's Notebook

St. Louis cut ribs are spare ribs that have had the excess cartilage removed. They are the length of baby back ribs but have more meat. If your butcher will not prepare them for you, use whole spare ribs or baby back ribs.

Sweet Potato Gnocchi
Applewood Smoked Bacon, Wilted Spinach, Toasted Pecans, Sage Brown Butter Sauce

(Makes about 80 pieces to serve 6 people 12 pieces each and some for the chef to taste)

Gnocchi:

2 lbs	Sweet Potatoes
3 cups	Flour
	Additional flour for the countertop (bench flour)
½ cup	Cornmeal (or semolina)

"It was my grandfather who inspired both my brother and me to become chefs. He spent his career managing restaurants. Most Sundays during our childhood were spent visiting my grandparents, and Grandpa always cooked Sunday dinner (different because it was at lunch time) for us. One of our favorite requests was gnocchi, (which, by the way, is pronounced NYOH-key although as kids we pronounced it YUCKY). Grandpa always made the dish from scratch and 'only from IDAHO potatoes and never EVER with eggs as they toughen the dough.' Eventually he taught me how to make the gnocchi. When we moved to South Carolina, I started making the dough from sweet potatoes using the same technique. They were an instant Southern hit. Here is how we did it."

For the Gnocchi: Preheat the oven to 375°F and coat a baking sheet with cooking spray. Prick the sweet potatoes all around with a fork to allow steam to escape from the skins. Place the potatoes on the baking sheet and roast until fork tender, approximately 20 to 30 minutes depending the size of the potatoes. Remove the potatoes from the oven and allow them to cool slightly. When the potatoes are just cool enough to touch without burning yourself, peel them and run the flesh through a food mill or ricer into a bowl. Mix in some flour with a spoon. As the mixture starts to hold together, pull it out of the bowl and onto a floured work surface. Knead in the remaining flour until 3 cups are thoroughly incorporated. Form the dough into a ball and cut it into 6 to 8 equal portions. Line a sheet pan with parchment paper and dust with cornmeal or semolina.

Still working on a floured surface, roll each piece of dough into a log shape about ½ inch thick (see the Chef's Notebook on the following page). With a knife or dough cutter, cut the logs into ¾-inch lengths. Next, take each piece and roll it off the end of a fork to put the characteristic lines into the gnocchi. As you roll them, make an indentation with your thumb, to help the gnocchi remain tender after being cooked. Place shaped gnocchi on the baking sheet.

Put a large pot of salted water on the stove. Taste the water for saltiness: it should be too salty to drink (like sea water). The potato gnocchi soaks salt from the water and seasons as it cooks. Bring the water to a rapid boil. Meanwhile, prepare a container of ice water for cooling the gnocchi after they are cooked. Add the gnocchi to the boiling water in small batches to prevent the water from cooling. When the gnocchi float to the top, remove them with a skimmer or slotted spoon and put them in the ice water bath to cool. When all the gnocchi are cooked and cooled, remove them from the ice bath and lightly coat them with olive oil. →

Sauce:

12 oz	Applewood Smoked Bacon, cut widthwise into short thin strips
½ lb	Butter
¼ cup	Fresh Sage Leaves, cut into strips
½ lb	Fresh Spinach, stems removed, leaves cut into thin strips
½ cup	Pecan Halves, toasted
	Salt and Fresh Ground Black Pepper

For the Sauce: In a large skillet, cook the bacon until it is crisp. Pour off the bacon fat and add the butter. Cook the butter until it starts to turn brown. Add the sage, spinach, pecans, and gnocchi to the pan. Cook, tossing occasionally until the gnocchi is lightly caramelized and hot throughout. Season to taste with salt and pepper.

Finish the Dish: Serve immediately on warm plates. If desired, garnish with shaved Parmesan cheese.

Pairing Suggestion: Pinot Noir (Russian River). The goal is to match the earthiness of the sweet potatoes and the nuttiness of the pecans and brown butter.

Chef's Notebook

1. Cut the dough.

2. Roll the dough into a log.

3. Cut the logs into gnocchi.

4. Place the gnocchi on a fork.

5. Press thumb into the gnocchi, making a dent.

6. Roll the gnocchi off the fork.

Lobster Cobbler
Summer Vegetables, Coconut Curry Sauce, Savory Lime Crumb Topping

(Serves 6)

Topping:

1	Lime
1 cup	Flour
1 tsp	Baking Powder
1 tsp	Salt
3 oz	Coconut Milk

Filling:

2	Maine Lobsters, 1¼ to 1½ lbs each (or substitute 1 lb cooked lobster meat)
2 Tbs	Olive Oil
¼ cup	Red Bell Pepper, diced
¼ cup	Green Bell Pepper, diced
1 tsp	Jalapeño, seeded and finely diced
1 Tbs	Fresh Garlic, minced
1 pint	Heavy Cream

1 cup	Coconut Milk
2 Tbs	Fresh Ginger, peeled and grated
1 Tbs	Lime Juice, fresh
3 Tbs	Yellow Curry Powder
3 Tbs	Cornstarch
2 Tbs	Water
1 cup	Sweet Peas, blanched*
1 tsp	Salt

*See the method on page 131.

"Chef Rob McCarthy (Soby's Chef from 2001-2006) describes this dish as 'a classic home-style cobbler with a twist—savory instead of sweet, with lobster and curry instead of fruit.' We describe it as New South Cuisine at its finest. Feel free to substitute crab or even chicken, pork, or tofu for the lobster. Whatever you use, it will be a huge hit."

For the Topping: Zest the lime into the bowl of a food processor. Juice the lime, and reserve the juice for the filling. Add the remaining ingredients to the food processor and pulse until the mixture becomes crumbly. If the mixture is too moist, add a little more flour until it is crumbly.

For the Filling: Bring a large pot of salted water to a full boil. Place the lobsters in the rapidly boiling water for about 7 minutes. Meanwhile, prepare a container of ice water. Remove the lobsters from the hot water and plunge them into the ice water. Remove the meat from the tails, claws and knuckles. Roughly chop the meat and set aside.

Heat the olive oil in a saucepan and sauté the bell peppers and jalapeño until soft. Add the garlic and cook 2 more minutes (do not brown). Pour in the heavy cream and coconut milk and bring to a simmer. Add the fresh ginger, lime juice, and curry powder. In a small cup, mix together the cornstarch and water to form a slurry. Stir in the slurry and bring the liquid back to a simmer. Add the reserved lobster meat and the peas.

Finish the Dish: Spoon the filling into six 6-ounce ramekins and cover with the lime crumb topping. Bake the cobblers at 350°F for 15 minutes or until the tops are golden brown. Serve immediately.

Pairing Suggestion: Gewürztraminer (New or Old World). The spiciness of the curry is cut and complemented by the Gewürztraminer's fruit and sweetness. Don't specifically seek out a sweet wine. Most Gewürztraminer is produced with just a tiny bit of residual sugar (slightly off-dry).

Chef's Notebook

For the peas, use fresh peas from your garden and cook them the day they are picked. If you don't know when the peas were picked or if they were picked more than a day or two ago, it may be better to use frozen peas. Peas are sweetest when they are harvested, because immediately after they are picked their sugar starts turning into starch. Keep in mind if you use frozen peas, they have already been blanched.

Seared Foie Gras

Old Poinsett Hotel Spoonbread, Caramelized Pineapple Butter Sauce

(Serves 6, with way too much foie gras!)

Spoonbread:

3½ cups	Milk
1 cup	Yellow Cornmeal
2 tsp	Salt
2 cups	Soby's Maque Choux, see page 134
2 Tbs	Butter
5	Eggs, separated

Butter Sauce:

1 cup	Sugar
14 oz	Pineapple Juice
¼ lb	Butter, at room temperature

Foie Gras:

1 lobe	Foie Gras (about 1½ lbs)
	Salt

"The Poinsett Hotel, located across the street from Soby's, was famous in its heyday for its spoonbread (a traditional Southern dish that is made from cornmeal and is eaten with a spoon). So, when we were writing the menu for our James Beard House dinner in January 2000, we decided to include a tribute to the Poinsett and give a Soby's twist to that original recipe. We served it with seared foie gras to highlight the dish's versatility. It was a huge hit."

For the Spoonbread: Preheat the oven to 350°F. Bring the milk to a simmer over medium heat. Add the cornmeal and salt and cook stirring constantly for 5 to 6 minutes, until thickened. Turn the heat to low, cover, and cook approximately 5 minutes. Add the maque choux and cook for 3 more minutes stirring constantly. Stir in the butter until it is melted and incorporated into the mixture. Remove from the heat. Whip the egg whites until they form firm peaks. Fold the yolks into the cornmeal mixture and then fold in the whites. Transfer the batter to a 2-qt casserole and bake uncovered until the batter is set (firm), 50 to 60 minutes. While the spoonbread is cooking, prepare the rest of the components so you can serve the dish as soon as the spoonbread comes out of the oven.

For the Butter Sauce: Place the sugar in a small saucepan over medium-low heat. Heat the sugar, and do not stir, until it turns light-to-medium brown. Whisk in the pineapple juice (the sugar will solidify, but don't worry, it will melt again). Simmer the caramelized pineapple juice until it is reduced to a syrup consistency, about 15 to 20 minutes. Remove from the heat and add the butter in small batches while swirling the pan to incorporate it. Serve warm. →

For the Foie Gras: Separate the two halves of the lobe by gently pulling them apart with your hands. With a sharp knife and a pair of tweezers, remove any veins that become visible when you separate them. Slice the lobe halves into ½-inch thick slices (about 2 oz each). Gently score the slices with a crisscross pattern using a sharp knife. Cover the pieces and refrigerate until it is almost time to remove the spoonbread from the oven. Heat a skillet over high heat until it is quite hot. Season the slices with salt and place into the hot pan, taking care not to overcrowd the pan. The foie gras creates its own oil as it sears. Be careful not to burn the oil. When the first side is seared, flip the pieces over and cook for about 1 minute on the other side. Repeat the process for a second batch if necessary (pour off and reserve the oil from the first batch).

Finish the Dish: As you finish searing the foie gras, place a serving of spoonbread on a plate. Top the spoonbread with a slice of foie gras. If the foie gras oil did not burn, whisk it into the pineapple butter sauce. Season the sauce with salt, and spoon some on top of the foie gras. As an option, serve with grilled pineapple. Bon Appétit!

Pairing Suggestion: Sauternes (France). Sauternes is the classic match the world over for the savory characteristics of foie gras. The foie gras is rich in flavor and fat while the Sauternes is acidic and sweet.

Chef's Notebook

Searing the foie gras can make quite a bit of smoke. If you do not have a strong ventilation system, you may want to consider searing it outside, if your grill has a side burner.

Items from the original Poinsett Hotel

FAMOUS POINSETT HOTEL SPOON BREAD

This recipe was given to Miss Lucille Benson (later Mrs. Robert Jefferson Walker) in 1941 by Mason Alexander, manager of the Poinsett Hotel.

1 quart water (4 cups)
1 pound cornmeal (4 cups sifted meal)

Bring to a boil. Add:
6 eggs
5 ounces butter (5 tablespoons)
2 tablespoons sugar
1 teaspoon salt
1 to 2 cups buttermilk
Pinch of soda

(Best if you separate eggs and beat whites. Mix all ingredients and add stiff egg whites.)
Bake in moderate oven.

Note: These measurements need to be adjusted for family size.

Entrées

128 · *Applewood Smoked Bacon Wrapped Pork Tenderloin*
Roasted Garlic Mashed Potatoes, Broccolini, Habanero Butter Sauce

133 · *Soby's Crab Cakes with Rémoulade*
Sweet Corn Maque Choux, Mashed Potatoes, Haricot Verts

137 · *New Orleans BBQ Shrimp*
Creamy White Cheddar Grits, Sweet Pepper Relish

141 · *Peachwood Smoked Pork Chop*
Creamy Pimiento Mac and Cheese, Southern Greens, Jalapeño Pepper Jelly

142 · *Beef Tenderloin with Shrimp Crépinette*
Charred Tomato Demi-Glace

149 · *Pan Roasted SC Farm Raised Striped Bass*
Green Tomato Nage, Seared Linguine Cake, Crawfish Relish

151 · *Braised Lamb Shank*
Zinfandel Reduction

152 · *Soby's Exotic Mushroom Meatloaf*
Horseradish Mashed Potatoes, Fava Bean Asparagus Succotash,
Caramelized Vidalia® Onion Jus

156 · *Tea Smoked Atlantic Salmon*
Wasabi Mashed Potatoes, Broccolini, Mushroom Soy Cream Sauce

163 · *Potato Crusted Grouper*
Crawfish Étouffée, Chive Crème

165 · *Pan Roasted Monkfish*
Lobster Mashed Potatoes, Asparagus, Roma Tomatoes,
Lobster Vanilla Bean Butter Sauce

169 · *Sautéed Skate Wing*
Exotic Mushroom Ragout, Roasted Garlic Cream, Snow Peas and Carrots

173 · *Caramelized Hickory Planked Salmon*
Spicy Crawfish Slaw, Pimiento Cheese Hush Puppies,
Roasted Shallot Aioli

Applewood Smoked Bacon Wrapped Pork Tenderloin

Roasted Garlic Mashed Potatoes, Broccolini, Habanero Butter Sauce

(Serves 6)

Pork:		Mashed Potatoes:		Broccolini:	
3	Pork Tenderloins	1	Mashed Potato Recipe, see page 135	2 lbs	Broccolini, ends trimmed
21-27 slices	Applewood Smoked Bacon	2 Tbs	Roasted Garlic Purée, see page 208	4 Tbs	Butter
					Salt and Fresh Ground Black Pepper

"Throughout history, some of the most popular dishes have used the main ingredient in more than one way. Examples range from Eggs Benedict (eggs with egg sauce) to the ever-popular Chili Cheeseburger. Our pork tenderloin wrapped in bacon has been one of the most popular dishes ever served at Soby's. I guess it's sort of like making sure a dish goes with a certain wine by using the wine in the dish. If the principle works, stick with it. For best results, prepare the pork one day ahead."

For the Pork: Rinse the pork under cold water and pat dry with paper towels. Remove all visible fat and silver skin with a sharp boning knife.

Tear a piece of 18-inch wide plastic wrap* 24 inches long. Lay the plastic wrap on the counter so the short side is facing you. See the Chef's Notebook at the end of this recipe for photos. Starting about 3 inches from the left side, lay the bacon slices vertically side by side slightly overlapping until you have created a "mat" equal to the length of the pork tenderloin (approx. 7 to 9 slices). Lay the tenderloin horizontally on the bacon about 1 inch from the bottom edge so the tenderloin lies across all the strips of bacon. Using the plastic wrap, tightly wrap the bacon around the tenderloin until it overlaps and no bacon sticks out. Be careful not to wrap the plastic into the roll. Continue to roll up the plastic until it is completely wrapped around the tenderloin. With both hands, grab the ends of the plastic wrap and twist them by rolling the log away from you on the table until the entire roll becomes tight. Fold the twisted ends under the package and wrap the entire package in another piece of plastic wrap to hold the ends in place. Repeat the process for the other tenderloins. Refrigerate for at least 4 hours and up to 2 days.

Preheat the oven to 400°F. Spray a roasting pan with cooking spray. Carefully remove the plastic wrap and place the tenderloins seam side down in the pan. Roast for approximately 30 minutes or until an instant read thermometer inserted in the center of the meat reads 145°F. Remove the meat from the oven. Loosely cover the meat with foil and allow it to rest for 5 to 10 minutes.

*18-inch plastic wrap is available at wholesale clubs (Sam's, Costco) or restaurant supply stores. If you can't get wide plastic wrap, use regular size wrap. Cut two sheets of 12-inch wrap 18 inches long and overlap them from top to bottom rather than left to right. Make sure you overlap them by at least 3 inches to keep them together when you are rolling the tenderloins.

For the Mashed Potatoes: Prepare mashed potatoes according to the recipe on page 135. In Step 5, add the roasted garlic purée. Keep warm until ready to serve.

For the Broccolini: Blanch the broccolini for 1 minute and shock (see page 131). Sauté the broccolini in the butter and season lightly with salt and pepper. →

Butter Sauce:

½ lb	Butter
2 Tbs	Water
⅓ cup	Heavy Cream
2 Tbs	Habanero Hot Sauce*
1½ tsp	Salt

*We use Marie Sharp's hot sauce. You can use any brand you like.

For the Butter Sauce: Place 4 tablespoons butter, the water, and the heavy cream into a saucepan. Place the remaining butter into another saucepan. Bring the first pan just to a boil. Gently warm the second pan on medium-low until the butter is melted. Remove both pans from the heat. Pour the contents of the first pan into a blender and blend on high. While blending, drizzle in the melted butter, hot sauce, and salt. Keep the sauce warm over very low heat until ready to serve.

Finish the Dish: Slice each tenderloin into six equal pieces. Arrange three pieces on each plate with the mashed potatoes and sautéed broccolini. Finish with the butter sauce.

Pairing Suggestion: Chardonnay (New World, oak-aged). A few oak-aged Chardonnays have slightly smoky overtones that are perfect for this dish. Ask your retailer for a recommendation.

Chef's Notebook

1. Lay tenderloin across bacon.

2. Roll tenderloin up in bacon, using plastic wrap to guide the roll.

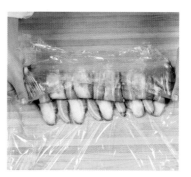

3. Take care not to catch the wrap in the roll.

4. Grab ends and roll to tighten.

5. Completely tight with ends tucked under.

6. Wrap with another sheet to secure the ends.

Blanching Vegetables

Have you ever wondered why your broccoli or green beans end up either brown and tender or green but tough? On the other hand, when you go to your favorite restaurant, the vegetables are the perfect balance of bright color and crisp tenderness. The difference is that chefs use a technique called blanching (boiling) and shocking (quick chilling). The technique requires some extra steps, but is well worth the effort.

Follow these steps for perfect vegetables:

1. Wash and cut the vegetable to the size needed for the dish you are making.

2. Fill a pot with water. Use a pot large enough to hold two parts water to one part vegetables.

3. Season the water with approximately 2 tablespoons salt per quart of water.

4. Bring the water to a rapid boil.

5. Prepare a bowl of ice water large enough to hold the vegetables.

6. Plunge the vegetables into the boiling water and boil until they have almost reached the desired level of tenderness (this time varies according to the vegetable per recipe).

7. Quickly strain the water off of the vegetables.

8. Plunge the vegetables into the ice water.

9. When the vegetables are cold, remove them from the ice water and store refrigerated until needed.

Soby's Crab Cakes with Rémoulade
Sweet Corn Maque Choux, Mashed Potatoes, Haricot Verts

(Serves 6)

Crab Cakes:

2 lbs	Lump Crabmeat
1 Tbs	Italian Parsley, chopped
½ tsp	Fresh Thyme Leaves, chopped
Pinch	Ground White Pepper
1 tsp	Old Bay® Seasoning
Pinch	Ground Mustard Seed
2 tsp	Worcestershire Sauce
½ cup	Panko*
¾ cup	Mayonnaise
1	Egg, whole
2	Egg Whites
	Olive Oil

*Japanese breadcrumbs, available in most supermarkets.

Rémoulade:

2 Tbs	Olive Oil
2 Tbs	Shallot, minced
2 Tbs	Capers, drained, chopped
6	Anchovy Filets, chopped
1	Lemon, juiced
½ cup	White Wine
¼ cup	Italian Parsley, minced
⅓ cup	Creole Mustard
2 Tbs	Worcestershire Sauce
2 cups	Mayonnaise

"When we decided that the restaurant would serve New South Cuisine, Chef David set out to design what would become the signature dishes. One month before opening (before any kitchen equipment was installed), we participated in Fall for Greenville, an annual three-day street festival showcasing a taste of our town for more than 100,000 visitors. This recipe won the People's Choice award for the best food item at the festival. The crab cakes are one of four items that have never been removed from the menu."

For the Crab Cakes: Gently pick through the crab and remove any shells. Mix all the ingredients together in a large bowl until thoroughly combined, taking care not to break up the crab any more than necessary.

Heat some olive oil in a large skillet. Scoop about ⅓ cup of the mix into the hot pan for each crab cake. Do not overcrowd the pan. Flatten with a spatula to approximately ¾ inch thick. Cook the cakes until they are brown on one side. Gently flip and cook on the other side until the cakes are heated through. Prepare two to three crab cakes per person.

For the Rémoulade: Cook the shallots, capers, and anchovy filets in the olive oil on medium heat for 1 to 2 minutes. Do not let the shallots brown. Add the lemon juice and white wine. Simmer until almost all the liquid is gone. Cool the shallot mixture. Transfer the mixture to a bowl and whisk in the parsley, mustard, Worcestershire sauce, and mayonnaise. Keep the rémoulade covered in the refrigerator until ready to serve. →

Maque Choux:

6 ears	Sweet Corn
1 Tbs	Olive Oil
¼ cup	Red Bell Pepper, diced
¼ cup	Green Bell Pepper, diced
¼ cup	Red Onion, diced
½ tsp	Salt
Pinch	Cayenne Pepper
½ tsp	Dry Basil
½ tsp	Dry Oregano
¼ tsp	Dry Thyme
½ pint	Heavy Cream

Mashed Potatoes:

1	Mashed Potato Recipe, see page 135

Haricot Verts:

1 lb	Fresh Haricot Verts*
2 Tbs	Butter
	Salt and Fresh Ground Black Pepper

*Haricot verts are thin baby green beans, available at many supermarkets.

For the Maque Choux: Carefully shuck the corn removing as much silk as possible (leave the stem intact). Cut the tip end off the corn to create a flat surface. Holding the stem, stand the corn on the flat tip and with a sharp knife, remove the kernels. With the back of the knife, scrape the cob to release the "milk" into a bowl. Place a sauté pan on high heat. When the pan is hot, add the olive oil and corn. Sear the corn until lightly browned on one side, then stir. Add the peppers and onions and reduce the heat to medium-high. Add the remaining ingredients and bring the mixture to a boil. Continue to cook, stirring occasionally until the cream is reduced and the mixture has thickened enough to coat the back of a spoon. Serve hot.

For the Haricot Verts: Cut off the stem ends of the beans, leaving as much length intact as possible. Blanch the haricot verts for 2 minutes and shock (see the method on page 131). Sauté them in the butter and season with salt and pepper.

Finish the Dish: Place a spoonful of mashed potatoes in the center of a warm dinner plate. Spread maque choux around the potatoes. Top with two or three crab cakes and the haricots verts. Serve with rémoulade on the side.

Pairing Suggestion: Chardonnay (Carneros). The extra acidity of the cool-weather fruit from the Carneros (southernmost parts of Sonoma and Napa counties) is what you are seeking with this wine.

Chef's Notebook

Your friends and family will love the maque choux and will want a second helping. For this reason, you may want to double the recipe. If you do have any left over, use it to make the spoonbread on page 123.

The Crab Cake recipe uses fresh thyme, which you can also use in the maque choux instead of dry thyme. When substituting fresh herbs for dry, use twice as much as the recipe calls for.

Mashed Potatoes

Mashed potatoes are one of America's most popular comfort foods and have been on Soby's menu since the beginning. At Soby's we serve our mashed potatoes smooth, not lumpy. This does not mean we use "instant" mashed potatoes, it just means we make our mashed potatoes using a large food mill. At home, you can use a smaller mill or a ricer to get the same smooth texture.

To make great mashed potatoes, you must follow a few simple but very important rules:

- Use a high starch potato such as an Idaho Russet or Yukon Gold.
- Cut the potato into even-sized pieces (so they cook in the same amount of time).
- Do not overcook the potatoes. When the potatoes hold their shape, but a fork can be easily inserted and removed, they are done.
- When the potatoes are cooked, drain them until they are dry. You may even dump them onto a baking sheet and warm in the oven to dry them although rarely is this step necessary.
- Work quickly while the potatoes are very hot.
- Do not let them cool.
- Process the potatoes through a food mill or ricer to make sure there are no lumps. Food mills and ricers are available at kitchen stores and some supermarkets.
- Always add hot liquid for flavoring.
- Do not over mix. Mix just enough to incorporate the flavor component and evenly distribute the seasoning.
- Add salt and pepper last, tasting as you add to avoid over salting. Potatoes need quite a bit of salt to bring out their maximum flavor.

Recipe: *(Serves 6)*

3 lbs	Potatoes, peeled and cut into even-sized cubes
1½ cups	Milk
¼ lb	Butter
1 Tbs	Salt (approx)
½ tsp	Fresh Ground Black Pepper (approx)

1. Cook the potatoes until they are tender.
2. Heat the butter and milk together until they are just about to boil.
3. Drain the potatoes well.
4. Pass the potatoes through food mill or ricer.
5. Stir in flavor or garnish components.
6. Add remaining ingredients gradually, to taste,

Instant mashed potatoes actually do have a good culinary use. One example is using them to crust fish. Just press your favorite fish filet into a layer of potato flakes and then place the filet into a hot skillet with a little olive oil. When the potato flakes turn golden, flip the fish over and cook through.

New Orleans BBQ Shrimp
Creamy White Cheddar Grits, Sweet Pepper Relish

(Serves 6, with some extra pepper relish)

Pepper Relish:
2	Red Bell Peppers
2	Yellow Bell Peppers
2	Beefsteak Tomatoes
1	Red Onion, cut into thin strips
1	Jalapeño, seeded and finely diced
2 Tbs	Fresh Garlic, sliced thin
	Olive Oil
2 tsp	Fresh Rosemary, chopped
1 Tbs	Dry Mustard
¾ cup	White Balsamic Vinegar
½ cup	Olive Oil
	Salt and Fresh Ground Black Pepper

Grits:
4 cups	Chicken Stock
2 tsp	Salt
1 cup	Stone Ground White Grits
¼ cup	Red Bell Pepper, diced
¼ cup	Green Bell Pepper, diced
½ cup	Red Onion, diced
½ cup	Heavy Cream
1 cup	White Cheddar Cheese, shredded
	Salt and Fresh Ground Black Pepper

"During the construction of Soby's, Chef David's friend Jimmy Richard visited from Lafayette, Louisiana, and prepared this New Orleans-style barbecue shrimp with David and Carl. The three immediately decided it would be on the menu when the restaurant opened. It has never been off since."

For the Pepper Relish: Start by grilling the bell peppers until the skins are well charred. Place them in a bowl and cover with plastic wrap. When the peppers are cool, remove the skin, stem end, seeds, and ribs. Cut the peppers into thin strips. Cut off and discard the stem end of the tomatoes. Cut the tomatoes into quarters from top to bottom. Remove and discard the seeds and cut the filets (with the skin) into thin strips. Place the garlic slices in a small skillet with a touch of olive oil and cook on medium heat, stirring constantly until the garlic becomes lightly toasted and fragrant, taking care not to burn the garlic. Put all ingredients in a bowl. Season to taste with salt and pepper.

For the Grits: Combine the stock and salt in a saucepan over medium-high heat. When the stock comes to a boil, whisk in the grits until smooth. Reduce the heat to low and simmer for approximately 20 minutes, stirring often to prevent the grits from sticking to the bottom of the pan. Add the peppers and onions and cook for another 5 minutes. Add the cream and the cheddar cheese. Season to taste with salt and pepper. →

Shrimp:

2 Tbs	Olive Oil
48	Shrimp (21–25 ct), peeled and deveined
1 tsp	Salt
1 tsp	Fresh Ground Black Pepper
½ cup	Red Bell Pepper, diced
½ cup	Scallion, sliced thin
1 Tbs	Fresh Garlic, minced
2 sprigs	Fresh Rosemary
1	Lemon, juiced
½ tsp	Pepper Sauce
1½ cups	Chardonnay
¾ cup	Worcestershire Sauce
¼ lb	Butter, at room temperature
¼ cup	Italian Parsley, chopped
	Salt and Fresh Ground Black Pepper

<u>Chef's Notebook</u>

Use the pepper relish as a condiment on just about any sandwich. You can make a quick hors d'oeuvre by grilling some baguette slices and smearing them with a little goat cheese then topping with the relish.

For the Shrimp: Heat the oil in a large skillet. Add the shrimp and sauté for 1 minute. Allow them to sear well before disturbing them. Add the salt, pepper, bell peppers, scallions, garlic, rosemary, and lemon juice. Cook 1 minute more. Remove the shrimp to a bowl while you finish the sauce. Add the pepper sauce, wine, and Worcestershire sauce. Simmer until the sauce has reduced by three-quarters. Put the shrimp back in the pan to reheat. Remove the pan from the heat and swirl in the butter and the parsley. Season to taste with salt and pepper. Serve immediately.

Finish the Dish: Place a generous scoop of creamy grits into a warm bowl. Spoon the shrimp and a good bit of the sauce over the grits. Add the pepper relish to the center of the bowl on top of the shrimp. Serve with a glass of wine and some crusty bread.

Pairing Suggestions: Amber-style beer or Chardonnay (California). Many traditional New Orleans-style barbeque sauces use beer as a base—but our recipe uses wine. Enhance the Chardonnay in the recipe by serving one of your favorite Chardonnays.

Peachwood Smoked Pork Chop
Creamy Pimiento Mac and Cheese, Southern Greens, Jalapeño Pepper Jelly

(Serves 6)

Macaroni:

1 lb	Ditalini Pasta
2 Tbs	Vegetable Oil
½ cup	Onion, finely diced
1	Jalapeño, seeded and finely diced
1 Tbs	Flour
1½ pints	Heavy Cream
12 oz	Sharp Yellow Cheddar Cheese, shredded
7 oz	Diced Pimiento
1 tsp	Salt

Pepper Jelly:

1½ cups	Sugar
⅓ cup	Apple Cider Vinegar
2 cups	Apple Juice
½ cup	Red Bell Pepper, finely diced
1 or 2	Jalapeños, seeded and finely diced

Pork:

6	Peachwood Smoked Pork Chops*

* For source of the smoked pork chop, see the New South Pantry.

Greens:

1	Sweet and Sour Greens Recipe, see page 51

"When Carl sees this dish coming out of the kitchen, he says, 'now that is Soby's food.' The macaroni and cheese gets a New South twist by using pimiento cheese, a traditional Southern favorite, and ditalini pasta. The sweet and sour flavor of the greens just screams New South."

For the Pork: Grill the pork chops until hot throughout, approximately 15 minutes, depending on thickness.

Finish the Dish: Place the mac and cheese and greens on a dinner plate. Glaze the pork chop with the pepper jelly and serve hot with extra pepper jelly on the side.

Pairing Suggestion: Shiraz (Australia). Choose a big Shiraz (the Australian name for Syrah) to complement the pork chop.

For the Macaroni: Cook the pasta in salted water according to the package directions. Cool under cold running water and reserve.

Sauté the onion and the jalapeño for 2 minutes in 1 tablespoon vegetable oil. When the onion is soft, add the other tablespoon oil and whisk in the flour. Continue to cook for 2 minutes, stirring constantly. Add the heavy cream and simmer for 5 minutes. Stir in the cheese until melted. Add the pimientos and the salt. To finish, add the pasta to the cheese sauce and heat thoroughly. Serve hot.

For the Pepper Jelly: Place all ingredients in a 1-qt saucepan. Simmer until the sauce is reduced by three-quarters, about 1 hour. The sauce will seem thin, but thickens as it cools.

Chef's Notebook

The leftover pepper jelly is good with anything grilled or fried. Try chilling the leftover macaroni and cheese in the refrigerator overnight. Then roll the macaroni into balls and bread them in seasoned bread crumbs. Fry them and dip them in the pepper jelly for a great hors d'oeuvre or side dish.

Beef Tenderloin with Shrimp Crépinette
Charred Tomato Demi-Glace

(Serves 6)

Demi-Glace:

3	Beefsteak Tomatoes
2 Tbs	Olive Oil
1 Tbs	Fresh Garlic, minced
1 Tbs	Shallot, minced
6	Fresh Sage Leaves, cut into thin strips
1 tsp	Fresh Rosemary, minced
½ tsp	Fresh Thyme Leaves
2 cups	Red Wine
8 cups	Beef Stock
	Salt and Fresh Ground Black Pepper

Beef:

	Olive Oil
3 lbs	Beef Tenderloin (Chateau Briand)*
1 lb	Shrimp (any size), peeled and deveined
1 Tbs	Soby's Creole Seasoning, see page 204
¼ cup	Italian Parsley, chopped
1	Egg, whole
1	Egg White
¾ cup	Heavy Cream
½ lb	Caul Fat*
	Salt and Fresh Ground Black Pepper

*See the Chef's Notebook for information about these items.

"When we opened Soby's Loft, we created several menus for guests to choose from, representing many different ingredients. The beef tenderloin quickly became the most popular entrée choice. Because this dish requires quite a bit of preparation, I suggest saving it for a very special occasion. The sauce can be made several days in advance and warmed for serving.

"When making mousse, it is important to keep everything cold. Chill your food processor bowl and blade with ice water and dry thoroughly before adding the chilled ingredients."

For the Demi-Glace: Heat a grill or the oven to 500°F. Toss the tomatoes in the olive oil. Place them on the hot grill or in the oven and cook until the outsides are completely caramelized, approximately 5 to 10 minutes. When the tomatoes are done, run them through a food mill. In a saucepan, sauté the garlic, shallot, and herbs until the shallot and garlic are soft and lightly browned. Do not burn the garlic. Add the red wine and simmer until it is reduced by half. Add the beef stock and slowly reduce by half again. Add the puréed tomato and season to taste with salt and pepper. Strain the sauce through a fine mesh sieve. Serve hot.

For the Beef: Heat a small amount of oil in a large skillet. Season the beef with salt and pepper and sear in the hot oil. Refrigerate while you make the mousse.

For the mousse, work with well-chilled ingredients, utensils, and bowls. Place the shrimp, creole seasoning, and parsley in a food processor and process until the shrimp is well puréed. Scrape down the sides of the bowl with a rubber spatula as necessary. For the next step, work quickly and keep going until the mousse is done. Stop the processor and add the eggs. Start the processor and drizzle in the cream as quickly as it can be absorbed into the mixture. As soon as all the cream is incorporated, stop the processor. Remove the mousse to a bowl and refrigerate it until needed. →

Preheat the oven to 375°F. In a clean and tidy workspace, lay a large piece of plastic wrap on the counter (you may have to overlap two pieces to make it wide enough). Have the caul fat, seared tenderloin, and shrimp mousse ready to assemble.

Spread a piece of caul fat on the plastic wrap. You can use several overlapping pieces, but the bigger they are the better. The caul fat must be as long as the cut of beef and wide enough to go completely around the beef. Place the seared tenderloin on the caul fat about 3 inches from the edge closest to you. Spread the shrimp mousse onto the tenderloin along the length of the far side of the beef until it is about 1 inch thick. Using the plastic wrap, tightly wrap the caul fat around the beef and shrimp. Be careful not to wrap the plastic into the roll. Remove and discard the plastic wrap.

Carefully place the beef in a roasting pan and season with salt and pepper. Roast for about 40 minutes or until a thermometer inserted in the center of the meat reads 125°F. Remove the meat from the oven and allow it to rest covered loosely with aluminum foil for about 10 minutes before slicing.

Finish the Dish: Slice the tenderloin into six equal slices. Serve it with the charred tomato demi-glace and your choice of side dishes.

Pairing Suggestion: Cabernet Sauvignon (Sonoma or Napa). Although shrimp plays a significant role in this dish, the beef takes priority for the pairing and gives you a great opportunity to serve your favorite Cab.

Chef's Notebook

Make arrangements with your butcher several days before you plan to prepare this recipe, especially around busy holiday times. Have your butcher cut a 3-lb piece from the center of the barrel (also known as Chateau Briand). Make sure all fat and silver skin has been removed. This cut costs more, but it is for a special occasion, so it is worth it. Next, ask your butcher for a couple nice pieces of caul fat. Caul fat is a thin layer of fat that provides a protective lining for the organs of the pig. It is white or pinkish and has no odor or flavor of its own. It is used to make sausages and to wrap meats. In this recipe caul fat is what holds the tenderloin and shrimp together. If your butcher cannot get it, you can order it at www.nimanranch.com.

1. Soak caul fat in fresh water and drain.

2. Lay a sheet of caul fat on top of plastic wrap.

3. Place seared tenderloin on caul fat.

4. Have the well-chilled shrimp mousse ready.

5. Spread mousse on tenderloin.

6. Cover one side of tenderloin with mousse.

7. Use the plastic wrap to roll the caul fat around tenderloin.

8. Trim off excess caul fat.

9. Season with salt and pepper before roasting.

Pan Roasted SC Farm Raised Striped Bass

Green Tomato Nage, Seared Linguine Cake, Crawfish Relish

(Serves 6)

Nage:

4 lbs	Green Tomatoes
2 cups	Vidalia® Onions, cut into strips
2 Tbs	Olive Oil
8 cups	Chicken Stock
¼ cup	Fresh Garlic, minced
1 Tbs	Salt
½ tsp	Cayenne Pepper

Relish:

1 lb	Crawfish Tail Meat
1 cup	Beefsteak Tomatoes, seeded and diced
½ cup	Yellow Bell Pepper, diced
4	Scallions, thinly sliced
½ cup	Fresh Basil Leaves, cut into thin strips
1 Tbs	Fresh Garlic, minced
1	Lime, juiced
½ cup	Olive Oil
1 tsp	Salt

Pasta Cake:

1 lb	Linguine Pasta
1 cup	Carrot, peeled and cut into thin strips
1 cup	Zucchini, cut into thin strips
2	Eggs
1 pint	Heavy Cream
1 cup	Asiago Cheese, shredded
	Olive Oil

"À la nage means served in broth. Chef Shaun Garcia, our chef de cuisine, served green tomato soup as the soup du jour one night when I happened to eat dinner in the restaurant. The broth was so flavorful and delicious that I immediately thought it would make a great sauce (nage) for a wonderful fish. If you can't get the striped bass, first complain to your fishmonger so he will bring some in and then substitute your favorite firm white fish. Make the pasta cakes one day in advance to allow them to set up."

For the Nage: Cut the stem end off the tomatoes and cut the tomatoes into large chunks. Sauté the onions in the olive oil until they are soft but not brown. Add the tomatoes, chicken stock, garlic, salt, and cayenne. Cook the mixture on medium-low heat for approximately 20 minutes until the tomatoes are soft. Purée the broth in a blender until smooth, then strain it through a fine sieve. Serve hot.

For the Relish: Mix all ingredients together. Refrigerate until needed. Serve chilled.

For the Pasta Cake: Cook the pasta in salted water until it is slightly al dente. While the pasta is cooking, whisk together the eggs, cream, and cheese. Place the vegetables in a bowl large enough to hold all the ingredients. When the pasta is cooked, drain it but do not rinse. Add the pasta and the egg and cream mixture to the bowl. Toss to combine thoroughly. Pour the pasta into a baking pan and press down to form a large pasta cake. Cover with plastic wrap. Set a slightly smaller pan on top and place a heavy object in the pan. Refrigerate the pasta cake overnight to set. Cut the chilled pasta into 4-inch diameter rounds with a biscuit cutter. Heat some olive oil in a pan and sear the cut cakes until they are golden and crisp on both sides and creamy and soft in the center. Keep hot for serving. →

Fish:

12	Striped Bass, filets, skin on
2 Tbs	Soby's Creole Seasoning, see page 204
	Salt
1 Tbs	Olive Oil
4-8 Tbs	Butter
4-8 sprigs	Fresh Thyme

Chef's Notebook

Striped bass is the official state game fish of South Carolina. However, due to various environmental challenges, not the least of which is over-fishing, it is not legal for restaurants to serve wild striped bass in the state. A great and sustainable option is the hybrid striped bass, which is farmed here in South Carolina as well as in other states in the Southeast. The hybrid bass is a cross between striped bass and white bass. The firm white flesh is lean, moist, and flaky. For other sustainable seafood choices go to <u>www.seafoodchoices.com</u>.

For the Fish: Season the bass filets with the creole seasoning and a pinch of salt on both sides. Cook the fish in batches to avoid overcrowding the pan, wiping out the pan between batches. Heat the oil in a large skillet. When it is hot, add bass filets, skin side down. Reduce the heat to medium. When the skin releases easily from the pan, gently turn the filets over. Add 2 tablespoons butter and 2 sprigs of thyme to the pan (for each batch you will need 2 tablespoons butter and 2 sprigs of thyme). When the butter turns brown, reduce heat to medium-low. Tilt the pan toward you so the butter flows to the side of the pan. Baste the fish with the brown butter allowing it to run off the skin and back to the side of the pan. Continue cooking and basting until the flesh is completely opaque and the skin is crisp, approximately 6 minutes. Remove the fish to a warm oven while you cook the remaining filets.

Finish the Dish: Place one of the pasta cakes in the center of a deep-rimmed plate or pasta bowl. Put one bass filet skin side down on top of the pasta, and another skin side up on top of that. Mound a bit of the chilled crawfish relish on top of the fish. At the table, add the hot green tomato nage to each bowl. For a flavorful garnish, drizzle hot sauce or sprinkle creole seasoning on the broth if desired.

Pairing Suggestion: Chablis (France). Just remember this is not a domestic chablis jug-wine! The elegant austerity of the classic French Chablis (made from Chardonnay) is a perfect accompaniment to the lightness of this dish.

UPSTATE SC: AN INTERNATIONAL REGION

Twenty-first century Greenville owes much to the cultural diversity its international residents bring to the community. In 1988, Michelin (France) moved its North American headquarters to Greenville. In 1994, BMW joined Michelin as a major international presence, when the German company located its US manufacturing plant between Greenville and Spartanburg. The popular X5 Sports Activity Vehicle and Z4 roadsters and coupes are manufactured here.

Upstate South Carolina also is home to international industry leaders ranging from Fuji (Japan) to Bosch (Germany), Dunlop Slazenger (United Kingdom), Royal Ahold (Netherlands), and numerous others. In 2004, Clemson University International Center for Automotive Research began development of a 250-acre campus in Greenville, which will attract even more global attention. And Maestro Edvard Tchivzhel, Music Director of the

Greenville Symphony Orchestra, hails from St. Petersburg, Russia, and has won international acclaim from appearances in England, Germany, the Czech Republic, Poland, Romania, Scandinavia, Australia and New Zealand.

This international presence has profoundly influenced Greenville, from adding exciting flavors to the cuisine, to simply reminding residents of the pleasures one can enjoy, sitting at a sidewalk café along the tree-lined walkways on Main Street.

Michelin's North American
headquarters in Greenville

BMW Zentrum museum at BMW Manufacturing in
Upstate South Carolina

Braised Lamb Shank
Zinfandel Reduction

(Serves 8)

"Would you believe we actually have a call list for this dish? In other words, we have a list of people we call if we are serving lamb shanks so they can drop what they are doing and come eat them... that tickles us pink! By the way, make these when you are having at least eight people for dinner or four people who want to take home leftovers. They are a bit of work (worth every second), so you may as well make a bunch of them."

Lamb:

8	Lamb Fore Shanks
1 cup	Flour
½ cup	Vegetable Oil
2 cups	Yellow Onion, diced
1 cup	Carrots, peeled and diced
10	Fresh Garlic Cloves, peeled
3 sprigs	Fresh Rosemary
750 ml	Zinfandel
½ cup	Tomato Paste
2 qts	Chicken Stock
	Salt and Fresh Ground Black Pepper

For the Lamb: Preheat the oven to 350°F. Dust the shanks with flour and knock off the excess. Place a large roasting pan on the stovetop. Heat the oil in the pan. When the oil is quite hot, sear the shanks thoroughly on all sides until they are brown (be careful not to splatter yourself when you turn the shanks). Remove the shanks from the pan. Pour most of the oil into a metal can or saucepan to cool and discard. Add the onions, carrots, garlic, and rosemary to the roasting pan. Cook until the onions are tender and lightly caramelized. Deglaze the pan by adding the wine and scraping the bottom of the pan. Simmer until the wine is reduced by half. Stir in the tomato paste and the chicken stock. Return the shanks to the pan. Cover the pan tightly with aluminum foil and place in the oven for 3 hours.

When the shanks are done, carefully remove them from the pan and keep them hot for serving. Pour the liquid from the roasting pan into a saucepan and bring to a simmer. Gently simmer, skimming the fat from the top until the sauce thickens slightly and most of the fat is removed. Season to taste with salt and pepper. Serve hot.

Finish the Dish: Serve with your favorite accompaniments. Roasted garlic mashed potatoes are a great match.

Pairing Suggestion: Zinfandel (Lodi or Amador County). As with the She Crab Soup and the New Orleans BBQ Shrimp, we can't help but recommend the varietal used to make the dish as the best accompaniment. Lodi and Amador Zinfandels are some of the most delicious available and great values!

Soby's Exotic Mushroom Meatloaf
Horseradish Mashed Potatoes, Fava Bean Asparagus Succotash, Caramelized Vidalia® Onion Jus

(Serves 6)

Meatloaf:

½ lb	Exotic Mushrooms (any combination of Shiitake, Cremini or Portobello)		3	Eggs
2 Tbs	Olive Oil		1 cup	Panko*
1 cup	Yellow Onion, diced		½ pint	Heavy Cream
1 Tbs	Fresh Garlic, minced		1 Tbs	Salt
½ tsp	Dry Thyme		1 tsp	Fresh Ground Black Pepper
½ tsp	Dry Oregano		½ cup	Creole Mustard
¼ cup	Worcestershire Sauce		¼ cup	Maple Syrup
2 lbs	Ground Chuck			

*Japanese breadcrumbs, available in most supermarkets.

"When I think of comfort food, the first thing that comes to mind is meatloaf and mashed potatoes. The problem with meatloaf is that whenever you order it, you never know what you will get. Believe me, there are as many bad renditions of the dish out there as there are good. Our meatloaf at Soby's is made with in-house ground beef tenderloin and wonderful cultivated exotic mushrooms. We use very few breadcrumbs, so the texture and flavor of the beef stand out."

For the Meatloaf: Remove the stems from the mushrooms. Clean the mushrooms using a brush to remove sediment or by quickly submerging them in water and agitating them vigorously. Remove them from the water as quickly as possible and dry on paper towels.

Sauté the onions in the olive oil until they are soft. Add the mushrooms to the pan and continue to cook for 5 minutes. Add the garlic, thyme, oregano, and Worcestershire sauce. Cook for about 2 minutes to marry the flavors. Remove the pan from the heat and refrigerate the mixture until cool.

Preheat the oven to 350°F. Spray a roasting pan with cooking spray. Place the beef in a large bowl. Add the eggs, breadcrumbs, and mushroom mixture. Mix thoroughly, kneading as little as possible. Over-handling toughens the loaf. Slowly drizzle in the cream while mixing to incorporate. Season the mix with the salt and pepper. In the roasting pan, form the loaf into a long tube shape. Press down along the center of the meat and repack it from the sides until the loaf has tightened up and no major cracks are visible. The loaf should be about 6 inches wide and 4 inches high. Bake for 40 minutes or until the internal temperature is 130°F.

Meanwhile, make the glaze by whisking the mustard and maple syrup together. Glaze the meatloaf and continue baking until the internal temperature is 150°F, about 15 more minutes. Remove the loaf from the oven and loosely cover it with aluminum foil. Allow it to rest for 10 minutes. The temperature should continue to rise to about 155°F. When ready to serve, slice into 1-inch thick slices. →

Succotash:

2 lbs	Fava Beans
½ cup	Carrots, diced
1 cup	Asparagus cut into ¼-inch slices, tips intact
2 Tbs	Olive Oil
3 cups	Fresh Corn Kernels, removed from cob (about 6 ears)
½ cup	Red Onion, diced
½ pint	Heavy Cream
1 Tbs	Salt
1 tsp	Cayenne Pepper
¼ cup	Maple Syrup
¼ cup	Italian Parsley, chopped

Mashed Potatoes:

1	Mashed Potato Recipe, see page 135
3 Tbs	Prepared Horseradish

Sauce:

1 Tbs	Olive Oil
1 cup	Vidalia® Onion, diced
½ cup	Carrot, diced
½ cup	Celery, diced
1 Tbs	Fresh Garlic, minced
1 Tbs	Tomato Paste
2 cups	Red Wine
4 cups	Beef Stock
1	Bay Leaf
2 sprigs	Fresh Thyme
25	Black Peppercorns
1 Tbs	Cornstarch
1 Tbs	Water
	Salt and Fresh Ground Black Pepper

For the Succotash: Prepare the fava beans by removing the beans from the pod. Blanch the beans for 30 seconds and shock (see the method on page 131). Next, remove the dull outer skin exposing the bright green bean. Blanch the carrots for 1 minute and shock. Blanch the asparagus for 30 seconds and shock. Heat the olive oil in a large skillet. Add the corn and allow it to sear until lightly browned on one side, then stir. Add the onions and cook until soft. Add the rest of the ingredients except the parsley and cook for 3 to 5 minutes until the cream has thickened slightly. Stir in the parsley. Keep warm until ready to serve.

For the Mashed Potatoes: Prepare mashed potatoes according to the recipe on page 135. In Step 5, add the prepared horseradish. Keep warm until ready to serve.

For the Sauce: Sauté the onions and carrots until well caramelized, stirring often. Add the celery and garlic and cook for 2 minutes to release their flavor. Stir in the tomato paste to coat the vegetables. Add the wine and bring the mixture to a boil. Simmer until the wine is reduced by half. Add the beef stock, bay leaf, thyme, and peppercorns and simmer until the sauce is reduced to 2 cups (about 45 minutes). Skim off any oil that comes to the top of the sauce as it simmers. Combine the cornstarch and water to make a slurry and drizzle it into the sauce. Simmer for 2 more minutes. Strain the sauce through a fine sieve. Season with salt and pepper.

Finish the Dish: Arrange the mashed potatoes and the succotash on a plate. Place a slice of meatloaf on top. Ladle the sauce over the meat and onto the plate.

Pairing Suggestions: Merlot or Cabernet Sauvignon (Sonoma or Napa). The key here is to buy a big, substantial wine to stand up to the substance of the meatloaf. This is a big dish! Serve a big red wine.

Chef's Notebook

We make the meatloaf in the restaurant with freshly ground beef tenderloin because we cut our filet mignons in house and have plenty of beautiful trim left to use. At your home, you probably do not have the same opportunity, so we recommend using ground chuck, which has a ratio of 80% lean to 20% fat. Ground chuck is the most flavorful ground beef that is readily available.

SOBY'S WINE PROGRAM

Danny Baker, Soby's current wine director, and Frank Kapp, Soby's first wine director, were reminiscing by email recently. Frank had just seen a recent *Wine Spectator* awards issue and couldn't help thinking back over the past ten years. "I was amazed at the number of South Carolina restaurants listed—almost sixty! Remember when Soby's achieved its first Award of Excellence? There were only fifteen or sixteen *Wine Spectator* awards in the entire state, and Soby's had won one in Greenville. We were all so excited, and not only us, but also our guests."

From winning a *Wine Spectator* award the first year after opening, to its list of over 550 selections today, Soby's has often surprised winery representatives. Wine dinners frequently included five or six courses with wine, for 150 to 180 people. Eli Parker of Fess Parker Winery once called a Soby's wine dinner "the mother of all wine events."

In 2003, Soby's list earned the Best of Award of Excellence—a distinction the restaurant has maintained each year since. In addition to the wine list itself, careful attention is given to staff education. Soby's servers participate in regular weekly wine training. From the time the restaurant was launched, staff has also been encouraged to travel to wine regions to obtain first-hand knowledge. In a recent twelve-month period, Wine Director Danny Baker visited California, Italy, and Australia.

Soby's parent, Table 301, has continued this emphasis as it adds other restaurants to its Greenville offerings. A total of five Certified Sommeliers (Court of Master Sommeliers) are on staff, as well as a full-time wine educator who is a member of The Society of Wine Educators.

Soby's Wine Director, Danny Baker

Tea Smoked Atlantic Salmon
Wasabi Mashed Potatoes, Broccolini, Mushroom Soy Cream Sauce

(Serves 6)

Smoked Salmon Marinade:

¼ cup	Teriyaki Sauce
¼ cup	Soy Sauce
¼ cup	Sesame Oil
¼ cup	Dijon Mustard
¼ cup	Water
¼ cup	Rice Wine Vinegar

Sauce:

½ lb	Portobello Mushroom Caps, cleaned and diced
½ lb	Other Mushrooms (Button, Shiitake, Oyster), cleaned and sliced
¼ cup	Olive Oil
1 cup	White Wine
½ tsp	Pickled Ginger, minced
1 Tbs	Fresh Garlic, minced
¼ cup	Smoked Salmon Marinade
¾ cup	Mushroom Soy Sauce*
1½ pints	Heavy Cream

*Available at any Asian grocery store.

> *"This dish is one of* Chef Rob McCarthy's *creations, which truly delights all the senses. The salmon is rich enough to stand up to the intense flavors of the dish, and the aroma coming from the smoker will drive your guests wild."*

For the Marinade: Whisk all ingredients together. Refrigerate until needed.

For the Sauce: In a large saucepan, sauté the mushrooms with the oil in small batches and remove them from the pan. Discard any excess oil. Add the wine, garlic, and ginger and simmer until the liquid is reduced by half. Add the smoked salmon marinade and mushroom soy sauce. Reduce the liquid by half again. Add the heavy cream and bring to a simmer. Return the cooked mushrooms to the pan and cook on medium-low for about 15 minutes, stirring occasionally. Serve warm. →

Mashed Potatoes:

1	Mashed Potato Recipe, see page 135
2 Tbs	Wasabi Powder
2 Tbs	Water

Broccolini:

2 lbs	Broccolini, ends trimmed
4 Tbs	Butter
	Salt and Fresh Ground Black Pepper

Salmon:

6 6-oz	Salmon Filets, skin removed
1¼ cups	Smoked Salmon Marinade, see page 156
1 Tbs	Green Tea
	Hickory Chips
	Salt and Fresh Ground Black Pepper

For the Mashed Potatoes: Prepare the mashed potatoes according to the recipe on page 135. Mix the wasabi powder with the water and add it to the recipe in Step 5. Keep warm until ready to serve.

For the Broccolini: Blanch the broccolini for 1 minute and shock (see the method on page 131). Sauté the broccolini in the butter and season lightly with salt and pepper.

For the Salmon: Marinate the salmon filets with the smoked salmon marinade and refrigerate for 1 hour. Smoke the filets using the green tea and the hickory chips until the filets are cooked through but still moist, approximately 10 minutes (see the method on page 49).

Finish the Dish: Place a scoop of the wasabi mashed potatoes in the middle of a dinner plate. Place a handful of the broccolini across the potatoes and top with the fish. Finish the plate with the mushroom soy cream sauce.

Pairing Suggestion: Pinot Noir (Russian River). With this dish, you are looking for a dark, smoky Pinot Noir to complement the preparation of the salmon.

THE SOBY'S STORY

LET'S FACE IT

Even before David Anctil joined the team at Soby's, he was well-known in Greenville for his work at Nippon Cultural Center, profiled in Southern Living magazine. Known to everyone as "Face," he has an exceptional ability to entertain, as well as inform, and that is exactly how he sees it. "There is no better stage in Greenville and no place I'd rather be!"

"Face" on stage at Soby's

Image from the Soby's Archives

THE SOBY'S TEAM

Soby's was built on a lot of trust and faith, not only from the guests who entered through the doors and allowed us to serve them, but also from the staff who took a leap of faith and agreed to join our team.

Soby's original team members still onboard ten years later.

∞∞

CARL: "The two keys to success are to surround yourself with good people and remember that 'excellence is not an act; it is a habit.' We hire for personality and train for experience."

DAVID: "Absolutely. You can train folks to do a job, but you can't teach them to be passionate. You can lead them, but you cannot motivate them. Hospitality has to be learned from an early age. This is not a job you can do just for the money. You have to have a built-in desire to take care of people, even above the desire to take care of yourself."

RODNEY: "One thing that sets Carl and David apart from many business owners is their philosophy that the restaurant business is not simply a career, but a way of life. That way of life should permeate every aspect of our being. In some ways, staff members really are not very different from the guests who eat in the restaurant. Both staff and guests want to be treated with respect and caring. Staff members also want to be heard and to feel they have input to decisions that affect them. And ultimately, I think most of us hope our work experiences will have a positive impact on personal development, as well as for the company as a whole."

∞∞

Continuing education is one of many ways Soby's contributes to team members' personal development. Staff has been given opportunities to work alongside many accomplished chefs who have visited Greenville, gaining experience and knowledge from them.

Over the years, several staff members also have taken specialized cooking classes at the Culinary Institute of America–both in New York and in California. In addition, staffers have traveled to restaurants including Charlie Trotter's in Chicago, and several operated by the Passion Food Hospitality Group in Washington, DC. Staffers have gone to Park City, Utah, to cook at the Sundance Film Festival; have headed off to Chicago to participate in the *Food Arts* magazine BBQ Cook-Off; and have cooked lunch for Senator Jim DeMint and his colleagues in Washington, DC. Staff trips to wine country in California,

Carl Sobocinski

David Williams

Blake Thompson

Vonderlyn Washington

Rodney Freidank

Danny Baker

David "Face" Anctil

Jorge Barrales, Sr

Janet Breaman

David "Soup" Dunning

At Food Arts magazine Chicago Cook-Off, 2007:

Left to right, front row: Mary Williams, Rae Sobocinski, Claudia Freidank

Back row: Rodney Freidank, David Williams, Shaun Garcia, Carl Sobocinski

Oregon, and France have had the added benefit of team building. Groups return from these ventures energized and ready to share their experiences and expertise with the rest of the crew.

Even on the personal side, Carl and David try to exceed staff expectations. Staff anniversaries are celebrated each year in conjunction with the restaurant's anniversary. Each staff member receives a gift commensurate with the number of years they have been part of the team. Gifts range from fleece pullovers and custom-designed sterling silver jewelry featuring the company logo, to cash, airline tickets, and trips to Las Vegas that include lots of personal time with Carl and David. Similarly, while Christmas is celebrated with a companywide "Secret Santa" gift exchange among team members, Carl and David distribute gifts of their own. But don't imagine their gifts are just the typical holiday turkey! They spend several months selecting the perfect gift for each individual, based on their knowledge of that staff member's life and personal interests.

∞∞∞

DAVID: "At a point the company was growing fast, it became harder than ever to really know what to get for so many different people. Thankfully, not long before, we had done a team-building exercise that included questionnaires on which people noted hobbies and interests. Certainly, they would provide some useful insights! And sure enough, there it was.

Based on the "Favorite Pet" section of his questionnaire, I thought I had the perfect gift for Mike, a pastry chef who loved his dog: a great dog bowl, with some biscuit cutters and mix to make his dog some homemade treats. I couldn't wait until Mike saw his gift. But did that ever turn out to be wrong! The dog he mentioned had passed away about 12 years before, and he was still saddened by the memory. He was mortified and I felt terrible. After I explained what I had intended, he was okay. Thankfully, I haven't made such a huge blunder since."

As the photographs of the team in this section show, ten staff members have been with the company for all ten years Soby's has been open. Thirty-seven have been on staff more than three years. Some folks who have left the company have gone on to open restaurants of their own—making us proud to have shared our knowledge and experience with them. Still others have left for what they thought would be better opportunity, only to be welcomed back with open arms when their move proved less successful than they had hoped.

With the support of the management team, and under the capable direction of Aimee Maher, Soby's staff continues to extend the "No-Walls Welcome" to both the guests and to each other.

∞∞∞

Pam Jordan *(opening pastry chef and former employee of The 858):* *"We have become a restaurant family...we've been to Chicago, San Francisco, and New York City. Carl and Dave have shown me a world of opportunity and helped me grow into a strong woman."*

Face *(perhaps the most requested server in the Upstate and another former employee of The 858, Face is still working his magic at Soby's):* *"I have had the best gig and have been performing on the best stage in the Southeast for as long as I have been associated with Carl and David."*

Dan Watters *(former Soby's manager):* *"At Soby's I have learned a lot...to treat people with respect, be honest, sincere, genuinely caring, to make people feel at home; and to enjoy my time at work and the people I work with."*

Chris Billoux *(former server, returned to his home in New Orleans):* *"Soby's is a one-of-a-kind enterprise. It is the only place you will work where the owners work harder than the staff. If they ask you to carry a bag to the trash, it's probably because their hands are full with two bags."*

A portion of Soby's current team (2007)

Potato Crusted Grouper
Crawfish Étouffée, Chive Crème

(Serves 6)

Étouffée:

¾ cup	Flour
½ cup	Vegetable Oil
1 Tbs	Soby's Creole Seasoning, see page 204
½ tsp	Dry Thyme
½ tsp	Fresh Ground Black Pepper
1 pinch	Cayenne Pepper
2 Tbs	Olive Oil
¼ cup	Red Bell Peppers, diced
¼ cup	Yellow Bell Peppers, diced
¼ cup	Red Onions, diced
½ cup	Scallions, thinly sliced
1 cup	Celery, diced
1 Tbs	Fresh Garlic, minced
14.5 oz	Diced Tomatoes (canned)
4 cups	Chicken Stock
1 tsp	Pepper Sauce
¼ cup	Worcestershire Sauce
1 lb	Crawfish Tails
	Salt

Chive Crème:

¼ lb	Fresh Chives
1 cup	Spinach Leaves
1 pint	Heavy Cream
	Salt

Rice:

2 cups	Long Grain White Rice
4 cups	Water
1 Tbs	Salt

Grouper:

4 Tbs	Olive Oil
6 6-oz	Grouper Filets, skin removed
2 cups	Potato Chips, crushed

"Grouper is by far the most popular fish in the Carolinas. This is certainly true at Soby's. Here is one of our favorite presentations. The étouffée is great on its own as well."

For the Étouffée: Make a roux by heating the flour and oil in a saucepan and whisking for approximately 4 minutes. Sauté the spices in the roux for about 1 minute then add the peppers, onions, scallions, and celery. Cook until the vegetables are soft and lightly caramelized. Add the tomatoes, stock, pepper sauce, and Worcestershire sauce, and cook for 15 minutes. Add the crawfish tails and cook for about 5 more minutes. Season to taste with salt. Keep warm until ready to serve.

For the Crème: Blanch the spinach and chives for 10 seconds and shock (see the method on page 131). Squeeze to remove the excess water and finely chop. Place the chives and spinach in a blender with half the cream and purée until smooth. Remove the mixture from the blender and whisk in the remaining cream. Season to taste with the salt. Refrigerate until needed.

For the Rice: Rinse the rice under cold running water. Place the rice, water, and salt in a saucepan over high heat and bring to a boil. Boil for approximately 5 minutes. Stir the rice once and then cover the pot. Reduce the heat to low and continue to cook for 15 minutes. Turn off the heat and allow the rice to rest covered for 5 minutes. Fluff with a fork.

For the Grouper: Heat half the olive oil in a large sauté pan. Press one side of each grouper filet into the crushed potato chips and place three of them, potato side down, in the olive oil. When the crust is golden brown, flip the filets and reduce the heat. Continue to cook the filets until the fish is completely opaque and flakes easily, approximately 8 minutes, depending on how thick the filets are. Remove the fish to a warm oven while you cook the other three filets using the remaining oil.

Finish the Dish: Ladle some étouffée into a deep-rimmed plate or pasta bowl. Place a scoop of the rice in the center of the étouffée. Lay the grouper on top of the rice and garnish with the chive crème.

Pairing Suggestion: Chardonnay (Sonoma, Napa, or Australia). This dish matches well with a substantial Chardonnay. Choose a big-flavored wine to complement the garlic, chives, and the grouper itself.

Pan Roasted Monkfish
Lobster Mashed Potatoes, Asparagus, Roma Tomatoes,
Lobster Vanilla Bean Butter Sauce

(Serves 6)

Lobster:

2 gal	Water
1 cup	Salt
2 1¼-lb	Maine Lobsters

Lobster Oil:

	Lobster Shells
	(see lobster preparation)
	Olive Oil
1 Tbs	Fresh Garlic, minced
4 Tbs	Tomato Paste
1 Tbs	Fresh Tarragon Leaves, chopped
½ cup	Brandy

Butter Sauce:

1	Vanilla Bean, whole
2 cups	White Wine
½ cup	Heavy Cream
½ cup	Lobster Oil
½ lb	Butter
	Salt and Fresh Ground Black Pepper

"Monkfish is a wonderfully sweet fish that also has a great texture. The taste of the fish is often compared to lobster—so much so that its nickname is 'poor man's lobster.' Since monkfish has become popular, however, I don't think it can be called 'poor man's' anything anymore. To accentuate the sweetness and texture of the fish, I like to serve it with Maine lobster. As for the vanilla bean, you'll just have to trust me. It truly is a wonderful combination."

For the Lobster: Combine the water and salt in a large pot and bring to a rapid boil. Place the lobsters in the boiling water for approximately 7 minutes. Meanwhile, prepare a large bowl of ice water. Remove the lobsters from the hot water and plunge them into the ice water, letting them cool for 5 minutes. Remove the meat from the tails, claws, and knuckles, and roughly chop. Reserve the shells for the lobster oil.

For the Lobster Oil: Using a strong kitchen knife or kitchen shears, cut the lobster shells into pieces.

Heat 2 tablespoons of the olive oil in a 4-qt saucepan. Add the lobster shells and sauté for 3 minutes. Add the garlic, tomato paste, and tarragon and stir to coat the lobster shells. Add the brandy and continue to cook until most of the brandy is evaporated. Add enough olive oil to the pot to cover the shells. Heat the oil to a gentle simmer and cook for about 20 minutes. Remove the pan from the heat and pour all the contents into a blender. Blend on high speed until the shells are made into a powder and disbursed throughout the oil. Strain the oil through a fine mesh sieve. Reserve for the butter sauce, mashed potatoes, and garnish.

For the Butter Sauce: Cut the vanilla bean in half lengthwise and scrape out the seeds with the back of a knife. Put the wine and the vanilla bean pod and seeds in a saucepan and bring to a boil. Reduce heat and simmer until the liquid is reduced by three-quarters. Add the heavy cream and simmer until the liquid is reduced by three-quarters again. Remove the sauce from the heat and quickly whisk in the lobster oil and butter. Season with salt and pepper. Serve warm. →

Tomatoes:

6	Roma Tomatoes
2 Tbs	Olive Oil
1 tsp	Salt
½ tsp	Fresh Ground Black Pepper
1 tsp	Fresh Garlic, minced
½ tsp	Dry Oregano

Mashed Potatoes:

1	Mashed Potato Recipe, see page 135
½ cup	Lobster Oil
	Reserved Lobster Meat

Asparagus:

2 lbs	Asparagus Spears
4 Tbs	Butter
	Salt and Fresh Ground Black Pepper

Monkfish:

6 8-oz	Monkfish Tails, cleaned (trimmed of anything that is not white)
	Salt and Fresh Ground Black Pepper
2 Tbs	Olive Oil
4 Tbs	Butter
2 sprigs	Fresh Thyme

For the Tomatoes: Preheat the oven to 350°F. Cut off the stem and slice the tomatoes in half lengthwise. Place all ingredients in a large bowl and toss to coat the tomatoes. Roast them cut side up on a baking sheet for 30 minutes. Serve warm.

For the Mashed Potatoes: Prepare mashed potatoes according to the recipe on page 135, substituting 1 cup milk and ½ cup lobster oil for the 1½ cups milk. Fold in the lobster meat right before serving. Keep warm until ready to serve.

For the Asparagus: Prepare the asparagus by breaking off the tough ends. Blanch for 30 seconds and shock (see the method on page 131). Sauté the asparagus spears in the butter and season with salt and pepper.

For the Monkfish: Season the tails with the salt and pepper. Heat 1 tablespoon oil in a large skillet. When it is hot, add three of the tails and sear until golden brown on all sides. Add half the butter and allow it to brown slightly. Reduce the heat to medium-low and add half the thyme. Tilt the pan toward you so the butter flows to the side of the pan. Baste the fish with the brown butter. Continue cooking and basting until the fish is cooked through and has a crispy exterior, approximately 10 minutes. Remove the fish to a warm oven while you cook the other three tails using the remaining oil, butter, and thyme.

Finish the Dish: Arrange the mashed potatoes in the middle of the plate. Place the asparagus spears and roasted tomatoes on the mashed potatoes. Add the monkfish and ladle the butter sauce around the plate. Drizzle a small amount of the lobster oil on the butter sauce.

Pairing Suggestions: Chardonnay (Sonoma or Napa) or Vermentino (Italy). Vermentino is a native Italian grape that makes a wonderful alternative to Chardonnay. Like most Italian varietals, Vermentino is an excellent food wine.

Chef's Notebook

Maine lobsters should be purchased live and preferably on the day they will be cooked. Look for the lobsters to be quite lively, especially if you are not going to cook them right away. As a general rule, if the lobsters were alive when you purchased them and they die, they should be cooked within 24 hours. If you feel you must kill them before cooking, do so by inserting a knife into the head between the lobster's eyes.

Sautéed Skate Wing

Exotic Mushroom Ragout, Roasted Garlic Cream, Snow Peas and Carrots

(Serves 6)

Cream:

Stock:

2 oz	Dried Porcini Mushrooms
2 cups	Chicken Stock, warm
1 lb	Portobello Mushrooms
	Olive Oil
½ cup	Carrots, diced
1 cup	Yellow Onion, diced
½ cup	Celery, diced
¼ cup	Fresh Garlic, minced
2 cups	Pinot Noir
4 cups	Chicken Stock
½ cup	Worcestershire Sauce
2	Bay Leaves
2 sprigs	Fresh Rosemary
25	Black Peppercorns
½ tsp	Dry Thyme

Sauce:

¼ cup	Vegetable Oil
¼ cup	Flour
2 pints	Heavy Cream
¼ cup	Roasted Garlic Purée, see page 208
¼ cup	Worcestershire Sauce
1 Tbs	Salt
½ tsp	Cayenne Pepper

"If you have never had skate wing, it is an absolute must. Don't be fooled by the beautiful white flesh that looks so delicate. The cooked filets offer a sturdy mouth feel and wonderful flavor that can really stand up to the bold flavors of exotic mushrooms, roasted garlic, and red wine in the dish."

For the Cream: Start by making the mushroom stock. Soak the dried porcinis in the warm chicken stock for about 20 minutes. Meanwhile, prepare the portobellos. Remove the stems, trim off the ends, and remove the gills from the caps. Brush off any visible dirt and roughly chop. In a large saucepan, sauté the onions and carrots in olive oil until they are caramelized. Add the celery and garlic and cook for 2 more minutes, stirring often so the garlic does not burn. Add the mushrooms (including the porcini mushrooms and their liquid) to the pot and then the wine, the 4 cups of chicken stock, Worcestershire sauce, bay leaves, rosemary, peppercorns, and thyme. Bring the mixture to a boil. Reduce heat and simmer for 20 minutes. Purée the mixture with an immersion blender. Strain the stock through a fine sieve and discard the vegetables. Reserve ½ cup of the stock for the mushroom ragout.

In the same pot, heat the vegetable oil and whisk in the flour. Cook on medium-low heat for about 5 minutes stirring constantly. Whisk in all but the reserved ½ cup of the mushroom stock, making sure there are no lumps. Cook for about 10 minutes. Whisk in the remaining ingredients and simmer for 10 more minutes. Taste and add salt and cayenne pepper. Keep hot until ready to serve. →

Mushroom Ragout:

1 oz	Dried Morel Mushrooms
1 cup	Warm Water
1 lb	Exotic Mushrooms (any combination of Shiitake, Cremini or Portobello)
	Olive Oil
1 Tbs	Fresh Garlic, minced
½ cup	Scallions, thinly sliced
½ cup	Pinot Noir
½ cup	Mushroom Stock, see previous page
½ cup	Roasted Garlic Cloves, see page 208
4 Tbs	Butter, at room temperature
¼ cup	Italian Parsley, chopped
	Salt and Fresh Ground Black Pepper

Skate Wings:

2½ lbs	Skate Wings, cleaned
	Salt and Fresh Ground Black Pepper
1 cup	Flour
6 Tbs	Butter
3 leaves	Fresh Sage
3 sprigs	Fresh Thyme
3 Tbs	Olive Oil

Vegetables:

1 lb	Snow Peas
1 lb	Carrots, peeled
1 Tbs	Olive Oil
2 Tbs	Butter
1 bunch	Enoki Mushrooms, cut to 2-inch length
	Salt and Fresh Ground Black Pepper

For the Ragout: Place the morels in a bowl with the warm water. Agitate the mushrooms for 20 seconds to free any sediment. Remove from the water, pat dry with paper towels, and cut into bite-sized pieces. Clean the other mushrooms, remove the stems, and cut the caps into bite-sized pieces. Heat some olive oil in a skillet. Combine all the mushrooms and sear in small batches, adding oil as needed. Remove the mushrooms and reserve. Pour off any excess oil. Sauté the minced garlic and scallions for 1 minute to soften the garlic, taking care not to burn the garlic. Add the wine and simmer until it is almost gone. Return the mushrooms to the pan, and add the mushroom stock and roasted garlic. Simmer until most of the liquid is gone. Stir in the butter until it is just melted. Keep warm until needed. Before serving, stir in the Italian parsley and season with salt and pepper.

For the Skate Wings: Cut each skate wing into 2-oz pieces. You should have three pieces per person. Lightly season the wings with salt and pepper and dredge them in the flour. Shake off the excess. Working in batches, sauté the skate wings in butter, with 1 sage leaf, and 1 sprig of rosemary for approximately 2 minutes. Be careful not to overcrowd the pan. Turn the fish over and saute about 2 minutes until the fish is completely opaque. The finished pieces should have a lightly golden and crisp appearance. Keep the fish warm while you cook the remaining pieces.

For the Vegetables: Cut the stem end off the snow peas. Carefully cut the snow peas lengthwise into thin strips. Cut the carrot into thin strips (you may want to use a mandoline). Sauté the snow peas and carrots in the olive oil until they are wilted but somewhat crisp. Add the butter and continue to heat until it is melted and has coated the vegetables. Remove from the heat. Toss the enokis into the warm vegetable mixture. Lightly season with salt and pepper.

Finish the Dish: Place a spoonful of the mushroom ragout in the middle of a deep-rimmed plate or bowl. Stack three skate wing pieces on top of the mushroom ragout. Place a nest of the vegetables on top of the fish. Bring the cream to the table in a pitcher and present the dish first without it and then pour the cream on right before eating to keep it hot.

Pairing Suggestion: Pinot Noir (California or Oregon). Surprise your friends that red wine can be served with a white fish, if the type of fish and the sauce are right for red. In this dish, the flavor of the mushrooms and roasted garlic paired with the richness of the cream make Pinot Noir a great choice.

Caramelized Hickory Planked Salmon

Spicy Crawfish Slaw, Pimiento Cheese Hush Puppies, Roasted Shallot Aioli

(Serves 6)

Slaw:

2 cups	Green Cabbage, shredded
1 cup	Red Cabbage, shredded
½ cup	Carrot, peeled and shredded
1	Red Bell Pepper, cut into thin strips
1	Yellow Bell Pepper, cut into thin strips
1 lb	Crawfish Tail Meat
½ cup	Sherry Vinegar
¼ cup	Sugar
¼ cup	Tomato Paste
1 cup	Mayonnaise
1 tsp	Cayenne Pepper
	Salt

Hush Puppies:

1	Yellow Onion, chopped
1 cup	Yellow Cornmeal
1½ cups	Flour
2 Tbs	Baking Powder
2 tsp	Onion Powder
½ cup	Sugar
1 cup	Cheddar Cheese, shredded
½ cup	Pimientos, diced
1	Jalapeños, seeded and finely diced
2	Eggs
½ cup	Buttermilk
	Vegetable Oil
	Salt and Fresh Ground Black Pepper

"For a while it was all the rage to serve food on a cedar plank, but we didn't think cedar was a flavor we wanted to add to our food (have you ever heard of cedar-smoked anything?), so we decided to use a hickory plank. At the time, we had to go to the lumberyard and have untreated hickory planks custom cut for us. You should have seen the lumberman's face! Now you can get hickory wood grilling planks at www.mainegrillingwoods.com. We branded the wood with our logo as a nice surprise when the guest was finished eating and it became a huge hit. Of course, the hush pups are a huge hit with or without the fancy presentation."

For the Slaw: Place all the vegetables and the crawfish in a large bowl. In another bowl, whisk together the vinegar, sugar, tomato paste, mayonnaise, and cayenne pepper. Season the dressing with salt as needed. Mix the dressing and the vegetables to your desired level of creaminess. Adjust the seasoning as needed and refrigerate until ready to serve.

For the Hush Puppies: Purée the onion in a food processor until it is smooth. Reserve. In a large mixing bowl, combine the cornmeal, flour, and baking powder. Make a well in the center and add the remaining ingredients and ½ cup of the reserved onion purée. Mix thoroughly. The mixture should be just moist enough to barely hold its shape (like wet sand at the beach). Heat oil in a deep fryer or tall pot to 350°F. Carefully drop the mixture by rounded tablespoonfuls into the hot oil. Cook for 2 minutes, turning as needed. Drain on paper towels and season with salt. Serve warm. →

Aioli:

6	Shallots, peeled
1 Tbs	Olive Oil
1 cup	Mayonnaise
1 tsp	Fresh Garlic, minced
1 Tbs	Worcestershire Sauce
1 pinch	Cayenne Pepper

Salmon:

6 7-oz	Salmon Filets, skin removed
6	Hickory Planks*
	Salt and Fresh Ground Black Pepper
1 cup	Sugar in the Raw (Turbinado)

*Available from *www.mainegrillingwoods.com*.

For the Aioli: Preheat the oven to 375°F. Place the shallots in the center of a piece of aluminum foil, drizzle with the oil, and wrap into a package. Roast for about 45 minutes or until the shallots are tender and caramelized. Place all ingredients in a food processor and process until smooth. Pass the mixture through a fine sieve. Refrigerate until needed.

For the Salmon: Preheat the grill to high. Place one salmon filet on each plank and season with salt and pepper. Place the planks on the hot grill until they are smoking. Reduce the flames on the grill to low and close the lid. Cook the salmon for about 8 minutes. Remove the salmon filets from the grill (on the planks) and sprinkle them lightly with the sugar. Caramelize the sugar evenly using a brûlée torch.

Finish the Dish: Place the planked salmon filet in the center of a plate. Serve with aioli on the side and extra hush puppies.

Pairing Suggestion: Pinot Grigio (Italy). An Italian Pinot Grigio with plenty of minerality is a wonderful food wine. If you want to be very specific, ask your wine retailer for something from Alto Adige. You'll find this wine cool and wonderfully refreshing during dinner and while preparing the salmon outside on the grill!

Chef's Notebook

If you do not have a brûlée torch, now is the time to get one. For a serious home cook, it is a great and versatile tool. You will have a lot of fun coming up with ways to use it in your cooking and the investment is minimal. Of course, the primary use of a brûlée torch is to caramelize the crème brûlée in the Desserts section.

Desserts

179 · *Soby's Ice Cream*

183 · *Soby's White Chocolate Banana Cream Pie*

184 · *Warm Ginger Molasses Skillet Cake*
Vanilla Ice Cream

187 · *Vanilla Bean Crème Brûlée*

189 · *Half-Baked Chocolate Cake*
Mango Sorbet

191 · *Maple Pecan Peach Cobbler*
Bourbon Ice Cream

192 · *Carrot Cake Cheesecake*

194 · *Sasparilla Pumpkin Cheesecake*
Blackberry Ginger Compote

197 · *Pan Toasted Vanilla Bean Pound Cake*
Blueberry Compote, Lemon Curd, Vanilla Ice Cream

199 · *Teryi's Eight Layer Bourbon Chocolate Cake*
Mint Julep Ice Cream

Soby's Ice Cream

(Makes 2 quarts)

Vanilla Ice Cream:

1 pint	Half-and-Half
1 pint	Heavy Cream
1	Vanilla Bean, whole
1 tsp	Vanilla Extract
9	Egg Yolks
1 cup	Sugar
¼ cup	Light Corn Syrup
Pinch	Salt

"At Soby's (and all Table 301 restaurants for that matter) we make our ice creams and sorbets on site. We believe no store-bought ice cream can match the texture, flavor, or wholesomeness of what we can produce right here. Soby's ice cream has no preservatives, additives, ingredients you can't pronounce, or nonsense. Here is the basic recipe and some variations so you can get creative at home. You will have to invest in an ice cream maker to have the most success. It is crucial to the texture of the finished product that the ice cream be mixed constantly during chilling and that it be as cold as possible before the mixing process stops and the ice cream goes into the freezer."

For the Vanilla Ice Cream: See the Chef's Notebook at the end of this recipe for detailed steps and photos. Put the half-and-half and heavy cream in a 2-qt saucepan. Split the vanilla bean in half lengthwise and scrape out the seeds with the back of a small knife. Add seeds, pod halves, and extract to the cream. Heat the cream until it is about to boil. In a separate bowl, whisk the egg yolks and sugar until they are light and fluffy. To temper the yolks, whisk one-quarter of the hot cream mixture into the yolks to warm them. Pour the egg mixture into the remaining cream on the stove. Heat the mixture slowly, stirring constantly with a high-heat rubber spatula, until it thickens enough to coat the spatula. Do not overheat, or the eggs will curdle and you will have to start over. When the cream has thickened, remove it from the heat and pass it through a fine sieve. Add the corn syrup and a pinch of salt. Refrigerate the base until cool. Churn in an ice cream maker according to the manufacturer's directions.

Pairing Suggestions: Serve coffee, espresso, or a small glass of something that complements the flavor of the ice cream—bourbon with the bourbon and mint julep ice creams, Kahlúa® with the chocolate, and so on.

Bourbon Ice Cream: Add ½ to ¾ cup bourbon to the vanilla ice cream base before cooling.

Mint Julep Ice Cream: Add 2 oz fresh mint leaves cut into thin strips to the cream while heating. Add ¾ cup bourbon before cooling.

Chocolate Ice Cream: Pour 2 cups of the hot vanilla ice cream base over 12 oz of your favorite chocolate and let it sit for 5 minutes. Whisk the mixture to melt and combine. Add it back into the base before cooling.

Fruit Ice Cream: Cook a pint of fresh berries with ½ cup sugar and purée in a food processor or blender. Add the purée to the hot vanilla ice cream base before cooling.

Herb or Spice Ice Cream: Add fresh herbs or spices (like mint or fresh ginger) to the cream while heating. Once the cream is flavored, strain out the herbs or spices before cooling and churning.

Chunky Ice Cream: Add chunky ingredients (chocolate chunks, candy pieces, and so forth) by stirring them in after the ice cream has churned and before it is frozen hard.

Many people ask how we get our ice cream to have such a wonderfully thick and creamy texture. The answer is practice. In cooking and baking, the thing that can't be replaced by a recipe description is gaining experience and developing instincts.

Be organized, measure accurately, and understand the method before starting. By tempering the egg yolks, you take them through the first critical stage of heating gently. For beginners, cooking the custard mixture to the desired thickness should be done slowly on low heat, stirring constantly. The thicker you make the mix (the more you heat it), the creamier the finished ice cream will be.

My goal is to take the custard mix as far as possible without curdling the eggs. You may make the ice cream a few times before you can comfortably push this envelope. There is no way of knowing how far that is unless you blow it at least once. Curdling the custard once gives you the experience to know when it is ready.

The next opportunity to affect texture is in the churning. The thicker (colder) you can make the ice cream before you stop churning it, the creamier it will be in the end.

The last detail that can make the difference between good and great ice cream is storage. Ice cream doesn't like to be melted and refrozen. A constant very cold temperature is best. Don't keep your ice cream in the door of the freezer. The temperature fluctuates too much. Keep it as far to the back of the freezer as possible. When you serve the ice cream, let it sit and soften for a few minutes before eating. The ice cream will be the perfect creamy delight you are hoping for.

1. Be prepared and organized.

2. Add cream and half-and-half.

3. Scrape the vanilla bean.

4. Add the seeds, pod, and extract.

5. Heat cream until it is about to boil.

6. Don't whisk egg yolks and sugar until cream is about to boil.

7. Remove one-quarter of the hot cream.

8. Temper the yolks by whisking in the hot cream.

9. Add tempered yolks back to hot cream.

10. Stir constantly until mixture thickens, taking care not to curdle the custard.

11. Mixture is ready when it coats the back of a spoon.

12. Strain through a fine sieve. Chill and churn.

Soby's White Chocolate Banana Cream Pie

(Serves 8 to 10)

Tart Shell:

1¾ cups	Flour
⅔ cup	Sugar
½ lb	Butter, cut into 1-inch pieces, chilled
1	Egg
1 tsp	Vanilla Extract

White Chocolate Pastry Cream:

1	Vanilla Bean, whole
1 cup	Milk
¼ cup	White Chocolate Chips
3 Tbs	Cornstarch
¼ cup	Sugar
¼ tsp	Salt
2	Eggs

Pie:

2¼ cups	Heavy Cream
½ cup	Confectioners Sugar
¼ cup	Crème de Banana
1 cup	White Chocolate Pastry Cream, chilled
6	Ripe Bananas
1	11-Inch Tart Shell, baked and cooled
	White Chocolate, thick piece for garnish
	Cocoa Powder

"If there is one item at Soby's that really needs no introduction, it would have to be the White Chocolate Banana Cream Pie. This pie has been the number one selling dessert on Soby's menu since the restaurant opened in 1997. Even though we call it a pie, we make it in a tart mold."

For the Tart Shell: Place the flour and sugar in the bowl of an electric mixer fitted with the paddle attachment. On low speed, add half the cold butter and mix for 30 seconds, then add the remaining butter. Continue to mix until all the butter is cut into the flour and the mix resembles sand. Lightly beat together the egg and the vanilla in a small bowl and add it to the flour and butter. Continue to mix until a dough ball is formed. If the dough does not form a ball after 1 minute, add a few drops of water. Remove the dough from the mixer. Wrap in plastic wrap and chill.

Preheat the oven to 350°F. Have ready an 11-inch removable-bottom tart mold. On a floured surface, roll out the dough into a ⅛-inch thick circle large enough to fit the mold. Press the dough into the tart mold. Refrigerate for 10 minutes. Bake the crust for 16 to18 minutes or until it is golden brown and crisp.

For the Pastry Cream: Pour the milk into a heavy bottom 2-qt saucepan. Split the vanilla bean in half lengthwise and scrape out the seeds with the back of a small knife. Add the seeds and pod halves to the milk. Heat the milk until it is about to boil. While the milk is heating, whisk together the cornstarch, sugar, salt, and eggs until smooth. Temper the egg mixture with one-quarter of the hot milk and then add it back to the pan. Whisk to combine. Continue to cook on medium heat stirring constantly. When the custard thickens, remove it from the heat and whisk in the white chocolate. Pour the pastry cream into a container and place a sheet of plastic wrap directly on top of the cream so no skin forms. Refrigerate until completely cool.

For the Pie: Whip the heavy cream until soft peaks form. Add the sugar and crème de banana and whip to very stiff peaks. Place the cold pastry cream into another bowl and soften by mixing it with a rubber spatula. Slice the bananas into the pastry cream and stir to combine. Fold in the whipped cream. Mound the filling in the middle of the tart shell and smooth it down to the edge. Carefully cut the pie into 8 or 10 slices before garnishing. Using a vegetable peeler, shave enough white chocolate curls to cover the pastry cream. Dust the top with cocoa powder. Serve immediately or refrigerate.

Pairing Suggestion: Moscato d'Asti (Italy). The light, fizzy, and fruity Moscato is a lovely match for the lightness of the white chocolate and banana cream.

Warm Ginger Molasses Skillet Cake
Vanilla Ice Cream

(Serves 8)

Cake:

2⅔ cups	Flour
2 tsp	Baking Powder
½ tsp	Baking Soda
1 tsp	Table Salt
4 tsp	Ground Ginger
1 tsp	Ground Black Pepper
½ tsp	Ground Cinnamon
½ tsp	Ground Allspice
½ tsp	Ground Cloves
1½ cups	Dark Brown Sugar, firmly packed
6 oz	Butter

1⅓ cups	Molasses
1⅓ cups	Milk
1 tsp	Vanilla Extract
¼ lb	Butter, cut into 8 slices
	Dark Brown Sugar
	Molasses

"We always bring out this dish in December. The smell of the ginger and cinnamon gets us thinking about the wonderful holiday season about to unfold. We make the cake in individual cast iron skillets. Serve it warm with some homemade ice cream!"

For the Cake: Stir together the flour, baking powder, baking soda, salt, and spices. Set aside. Place the brown sugar, 6 oz butter, and molasses in a saucepan and heat until the butter is melted. Stir the sugar and butter mixture into the dry ingredient mix and add the milk and vanilla.

Preheat the oven to 350°F. Spray eight 6½-inch skillets with cooking spray. Place a pat of butter, a teaspoon of brown sugar, and a teaspoon of molasses in each skillet. Place the skillets on baking sheets and heat in the oven until the butter is melted. Remove the skillets from the oven and fill with the batter. Bake the skillets on the baking sheets for approximately 20 minutes.

Serve warm with homemade Vanilla Ice Cream (see page 179).

Pairing Suggestions: Vanilla-bean infused Cognac, Tawny Port, or coffee. At Christmas, eggnog is the perfect indulgence.

Chef's Notebook

This recipe uses eight 6½-inch cast iron skillets. The skillets are inexpensive and are available at <u>*www.amazon.com.*</u>

Vanilla Bean Crème Brûlée

(Serves 8)

Crème Brûlée:

1 pint	Half-and-Half, divided
1 pint	Heavy Cream
1	Vanilla Bean, whole
14	Egg Yolks
1 cup	Sugar in the Raw (Turbinado)

"Over the years we have had many different flavors of crème brûlée on the menu at Soby's. However, no matter what glorious creation our pastry team comes up with, it seems that our customers want the original vanilla bean. Crème brûlée is one of the most luscious, decadent, mouthwatering desserts you can eat and surprisingly, one of the easiest to prepare."

For the Crème Brûlée: Place the heavy cream and half-and-half into a saucepan. Split the vanilla bean in half lengthwise and scrape out the seeds with the back of a small knife. Add the seeds and pod halves to the pan and stir to distribute the beans and break up any clumps. Heat the cream until it is about to boil. While the cream is heating, whisk together the sugar and egg yolks. Remove the cream from the heat. Temper the yolks with one-quarter of the hot liquid and add the mixture back to the pan. Whisk to combine. Strain the mixture through a fine sieve and allow it to cool.

Preheat the oven to 325°F. Pour the mix into eight 6-oz ramekins and place them in a baking dish. Fill the baking dish with warm water halfway to the top of the ramekins. Bake for 25 minutes or until the custard is set. The custard should shimmer but not move significantly when shaken lightly. Remove the brûlées from the oven and chill until ready to serve.

Immediately before serving, dust the top of each brûlée with Sugar in the Raw. Pour off any excess sugar because it will burn before caramelizing evenly. Using a brûlée torch, heat the sugar until it is evenly browned. Serve immediately.

Pairing Suggestions: Tawny Port or a botrytis-affected wine. Known affectionately as the "noble rot," botrytis is a fungus on the skin of the grapes that causes dramatically increased concentration of sugars. It also imparts a completely unique flavor to wine, a flavor that accompanies crème brûlée well.

Half-Baked Chocolate Cake
Mango Sorbet

(Serves 8)

Cake:

¼ lb	Butter
⅔ cup	Bittersweet Chocolate, chips or small pieces
2	Eggs, whole
2	Egg Yolks
¼ cup	Sugar
2 tsp	Flour, sifted

Sorbet:

5	Mangoes, very ripe
2	Oranges
¾ cup	Sugar
Pinch	Salt
1	Egg White

"I like to think of chocolate as 'kid's chocolate' and 'adult's chocolate.' This cake is certainly adult's chocolate. The flavor is deep and rich and is balanced by the mango sorbet. When you cut into the cake, it should ooze out onto the plate and create a very large smile."

For the Cake: Preheat the oven to 350°F. Spray eight 4-oz ramekins with cooking spray. Melt the butter and chocolate over a water bath. Using an electric mixer, whip the eggs, yolks, and sugar until they are pale, thick, and almost tripled in volume (ribbon stage). Stir together the butter and chocolate until smooth and well combined. Gently fold one-quarter of the egg mixture into the chocolate with a rubber spatula. Next, fold in the rest of the egg mixture, taking care to incorporate all the ingredients while beating as little air out of the eggs as possible. Once the eggs are almost completely incorporated, fold in the sifted flour. Spoon the mixture into the ramekins and bake for exactly 15 minutes. The cakes will have the appearance of a soufflé and be very soft in the center. Remove them from the oven and let them sit for 5 minutes. Invert each ramekin onto an individual servng plate and remove the ramekin. Serve with homemade mango sorbet.

For the Sorbet: Peel the mangoes and carefully cut the flesh off of the pit. Cut the fruit into chunks and reserve. Zest and juice the oranges into a saucepan. Add the sugar. Heat the liquid, stirring occasionally until the sugar melts. Blend the orange juice mixture and mangoes until smooth. Add a pinch of salt. Whisk the egg white and add to the fruit purée. Process the sorbet in an ice cream maker according to the manufacturer's directions.

Pairing Suggestion: Brachetto d'Acqui. This is a slightly sweet, dark rosé sparkling wine that is Chef Rodney's favorite accompaniment for this dessert!

Maple Pecan Peach Cobbler
Bourbon Ice Cream

(Serves 6 to 8)

Filling:

1 cup	Pecan Pieces
¼ tsp	Salt
¼ lb	Butter
¼ cup	Light Brown Sugar, firmly packed
1 cup	Maple Syrup
2	Eggs
2 cups	Fresh Peaches, peeled and chopped

Crust:

6 Tbs	Butter
1 cup	Flour
1 cup	Sugar
1 tsp	Baking Powder
½ tsp	Baking Soda
¼ tsp	Salt
1 cup	Buttermilk

"How many ways can we say Welcome to South Carolina? How about Cobbler, Pecans, Peaches, and Bourbon all in the same dessert? 'Y'all come back now, y'hear.' All right, I am pretty sure there is an unwritten law about not saying that in Soby's...EVER!"

For the Filling: Season the pecan pieces with the salt and toast in a 375°F oven until brown and aromatic, approximately 10 minutes. Cream together the butter and sugar. Add the syrup and eggs and mix well. Stir in the nuts and peaches. Set the mixture aside while you prepare the crust.

For the Crust: Preheat the oven to 375°F. Place the butter in the bottom of a 2-qt casserole dish and melt it in the oven. Mix the flour, sugar, baking powder, baking soda, and salt. Stir in the buttermilk. Pour the batter into the casserole with the melted butter. Pour the cobbler filling over the crust batter and bake for 45 minutes or until the top is golden brown and crisp. Serve warm, topped with bourbon ice cream (see page 179).

Pairing Suggestions: Honey-sweetened bourbon, Tawny Port, or coffee. Staff consensus on the Southern favorite for this dish is honey-sweetened bourbon.

Carrot Cake Cheesecake

(Serves 8)

Carrot Cake:

1 cup	Flour
2 tsp	Baking Powder
¼ tsp	Baking Soda
1 tsp	Ground Cinnamon
2	Eggs
1 cup	Sugar
¾ cup	Vegetable Oil
1 cup	Carrot, peeled and finely grated
½ cup	Pecan Pieces

Cheesecake:

1 lb	Cream Cheese, at room temperature
1 cup	Sugar
¾ cup	Sour Cream
1 Tbs	Cornstarch
3	Eggs
1 tsp	Vanilla Extract
2 tsp	Lemon Juice, fresh squeezed

"Pastry Chef Teryi Youngblood recently told me the story of how she had the idea for this wonderful dessert: 'I love carrot cake and was eating some with my sister. I couldn't tell you where, cloud nine probably because I was sleeping. I looked at her and said, "You know, I love carrot cake but there is never enough cream cheese icing." So in my dream I made the cheesecake and it was goooooood!!! The next day I made it for Soby's and the rest is history.' Do YOU dream in flavors?"

For the Carrot Cake: Preheat the oven to 350°F. Line the bottom of a 9-inch spring form pan with wax paper. Wrap the outside of the pan with aluminum foil. Whisk together the flour, baking powder, baking soda, and cinnamon, and set them aside. Using an electric mixer, combine the eggs, sugar, and oil and beat on medium speed until the mixture becomes thick and pale (about 2 minutes). Fold in the dry ingredients. When they are mostly combined, beat on high for 2 more minutes. Fold in the carrots and pecans. Pour the mixture into the prepared pan. Bake for 15 minutes or until a toothpick inserted into the center of the cake comes out clean. Remove from the oven and allow the cake to cool at room temperature. Do not remove the spring form pan. Meanwhile, prepare the cheesecake layer.

For the Cheesecake: Preheat the oven to 350°F. Place the cream cheese and sugar in the bowl of a food processor. Process until smooth, scraping down the sides as needed (do not over-process and incorporate too much air). Add the sour cream and process until combined. Add the eggs one at a time, using the pulse button to incorporate. Scrape down the sides of the bowl as needed. Finally, stir in the vanilla and lemon juice. With the cooled carrot cake still in the pan, pour the cheesecake batter on top. Place the cake in a large baking pan and fill the pan with warm water halfway to the top of the cake pan. Bake for 20 to 30 minutes. The cheesecake layer should shimmer, but not roll when shaken lightly. Remove the cake from the oven and let it cool completely in the water bath at room temperature. Remove the cake from the water bath and from the springform pan. Refrigerate for at least 4 hours before serving. Garnish with candied pecans and fried carrot ribbons, if desired.

Pairing Suggestions: Late Harvest Riesling or Icewine. Icewine (also called Ice Wine or Eiswein) is a highly concentrated dessert wine with an extraordinary balance of sweetness and acidity, which allows the wine to complement desserts beautifully.

Sasparilla Pumpkin Cheesecake
Blackberry Ginger Compote

(Serves 8)

Crust:

2 cups	Ginger Snap Crumbs, (about 45 store-bought ginger snaps)
4 Tbs	Butter, melted
½ cup	Sugar

Filling:

1 lb	Cream Cheese, at room temperature
1 cup	Light Brown Sugar, firmly packed
2 Tbs	Cornstarch
1 cup	Sour Cream
1½ cups	Pumpkin Purée
4	Eggs
2 tsp	Vanilla Extract
1 tsp	Ground Cinnamon
¼ tsp	Ground Nutmeg
¼ cup	Root Beer Schnapps

Compote:

1 Tbs	Cornstarch
½ cup	Sugar
¼ cup	Orange Juice
2 cups	Blackberries
½ tsp	Fresh Ginger, peeled and grated

"Make this recipe in the late summer or early fall when fresh blackberries are still available and folks are just starting to think about pumpkins and the beautiful fall harvest that is on the horizon."

For the Crust: Line a 9-inch spring form pan with wax paper and spray the sides and paper-lined bottom with cooking spray. Wrap the outside of the pan with aluminum foil. Mix the crumbs, melted butter, and sugar together. Press the crumb mixture firmly into the bottom and sides of the pan to make the crust. Set aside until the filling is made.

For the Filling: Preheat the oven to 350°F. Place the cream cheese, sugar, and cornstarch in a food processor and process until smooth. Scrape down the sides with a rubber spatula and add the sour cream and pumpkin. Continue to process, adding the eggs one at a time and scraping the sides after each one. Stir in the vanilla, the spices, and the schnapps. Pour the batter into the prepared crust. Place the spring form pan into a large baking pan. Fill the baking pan with warm water halfway to the top of the cake pan. Bake for 45 minutes or until the cake is set. Remove the pan from the oven and let it cool. Remove the cake from the spring form pan and refrigerate at least 4 hours. Serve with the compote and top with whipped cream.

For the Compote: Combine all ingredients in a saucepan. Cook over medium heat, swirling the pan occasionally until the mixture has boiled and becomes thick and clear. Remove from the heat and refrigerate until ready to serve.

Pairing Suggestion: Late Harvest Gewürztraminer. The slight spiciness of Gewürztraminer matches the spiciness of the pumpkin cheesecake well.

Pan Toasted Vanilla Bean Pound Cake
Blueberry Compote, Lemon Curd, Vanilla Ice Cream

(Serves 6 to 8)

Pound Cake:

½ lb	Butter, at room temperature
½ lb	Cream Cheese, at room temperature
2 cups	Sugar
1	Vanilla Bean, whole
6	Eggs
2 cups	Flour
1 tsp	Baking Powder

Blueberry Compote:

1 Tbs	Cornstarch
½ cup	Sugar
¼ cup	Water
2 cups	Fresh Blueberries

Lemon Curd:

3	Lemons (large)
¾ cup	Sugar
¼ cup	Butter
8	Egg Yolks

*"**Warm pound cake** and ice cream together is a great Southern dessert combination. Lemon and blueberry is a great anything combination! When put all together, you have a simple-to-make dessert that will please your family and guests very much."*

For the Pound Cake: Preheat the oven to 350°F. Spray the inside of a 10 x 3½-inch bundt pan with cooking spray and dust it with flour. Knock out any excess flour. Place the butter and cream cheese in the bowl of an electric mixer and mix using the paddle attachment until well combined. Add the sugar, ½ cup at a time, mixing between additions. Beat for 5 minutes, scraping down the sides of the bowl occasionally with a rubber spatula. Split the vanilla bean in half lengthwise and scrape out the seeds with the back of a small knife. Add the vanilla seeds to the batter and mix in the eggs one at a time. Remove the bowl from the mixer and fold in the flour and baking powder. Return the bowl to the mixer and mix until smooth. Pour the batter into the pan. Bake for 30 to 45 minutes, until a toothpick inserted into the center of the cake comes out clean. Allow the cake to rest for 10 minutes. Remove the cake from the pan and let it cool competely on a wire rack.

For the Compote: Combine all ingredients in a saucepan. Add the berries to the sugar mixture and stir. Cook over medium heat, swirling the pan occasionally until the mixture has boiled and becomes thick and clear. Remove from the heat and refrigerate until ready to serve.

For the Lemon Curd: Zest and juice the lemons into a saucepan (should yield about ¼ cup juice). Add the sugar and butter. Heat the mixture until it boils. Place the egg yolks in a bowl large enough to hold all the ingredients. Strain the hot liquid through a fine sieve and quickly whisk it into the yolks. Return the mixture to the saucepan and cook on low heat, stirring constantly until the mixture thickens and coats the back of a spoon. Remove the curd from the heat. Pour the curd into a container and place a sheet of plastic wrap directly on top of the curd so no skin forms. Refrigerate until completely cool.

Finish the Dish: Slice the cake into ½-inch thick pieces. Toast in a skillet with a small amount of butter until the outside is golden and crisp. Serve with lemon curd, vanilla ice cream (see page 179), and blueberry compote.

Pairing Suggestions: Limoncello (Italy) or Tawny Port. Limoncello is a bright yellow lemon liqueur that complements the lemon curd and blueberries in the recipe. Tawny Port is an alternative, a great match any time for pound cake.

Teryi's Eight Layer Bourbon Chocolate Cake

Mint Julep Ice Cream

(Makes 20 ¾-inch thick slices)

Cake:

18	Egg Whites
2¾ cups	Sugar
26	Egg Yolks
1½ cups	Cocoa Powder
¼ cup	Flour
¼ lb	Butter, melted

Buttercream:

8 oz	White Chocolate
3½ cups	Sugar
20	Egg Whites
½ tsp	Table Salt
2½ lbs	Butter, cut into 1-oz pieces, at room temperature
¼ cup	Bourbon

"This is it, Teryi's pièce de résistance. It all came about when Carl asked Teryi to create a chocolate cake that would make him proud to have on the Soby's menu. It started out to be a Bailey's and Chocolate cake, but then, as she put it, her 'bourbon bone' kicked in and the rest is history. The classic Southern flavor of the mint julep was just a natural progression. Make the cake and allow it to cool. While it is cooling, make the buttercream. Assemble the cake, and then make the glaze and finish."

For the Cake: Preheat the oven to 375°F. Spray four 10 x 15 x ½-inch baking sheets with cooking spray. Line the bottoms with wax paper and spray again.

Using an electric mixer, whip the egg whites and sugar to soft peaks. The whites should be glossy. With the mixer on low speed, add the yolks and mix to combine. Sift the cocoa powder and flour together and gently fold them into the egg mixture using a rubber spatula. Fold in the melted butter. Immediately divide the batter equally into the four baking sheets and spread evenly. Bake for 14 minutes. Allow to cool unrefrigerated.

For the Buttercream: Melt the chocolate and set aside. Combine the sugar and egg whites in the bowl of an electric mixer and place over a water bath on medium-low heat. Stir constantly until the egg-white mixture reaches 140°F and the sugar is completely dissolved. Remove from the heat and whip on high until the mixture cools. The egg whites should be thick and glossy and have doubled in volume. Continue whipping and add the butter, one piece at a time. Do not add the next piece until the current one is incorporated or the emulsion will break. If this happens, just continue to whip and the cream will come back together. Once it does, continue to add the butter slowly until it is all incorporated. Stir in the melted chocolate and the bourbon. →

Glaze:

1 lb	Bittersweet Chocolate Chips (or small pieces)
¾ lb	Butter
¼ cup	Light Corn Syrup

Assemble the Cake: You will need one cake board cut to 5 x 15 inches.

Spread a ¼-inch thick layer of buttercream on one of the cakes. Invert one of the other cakes on top of the buttercream and remove the wax paper. Spread a ¼-inch layer of buttercream on that layer. Repeat this process two more times, creating a four-layer cake. Refrigerate the cake for at least 1 hour. Cover the remaining buttercream with plastic wrap and leave it on the counter until needed again.

When the cake has thoroughly chilled, cut it in half lengthwise. Spread a ¼-inch thick layer of buttercream on top of one of the halves and place that half on the cake board. Carefully place the other half on top. Spread a thin layer of buttercream on all sides of the cake. This layer is called a crumb coating and is used to seal the sides of the cake before glazing. Crumb coating should be so thin you can almost see through it. Cool the cake in the refrigerator for at least 1 hour.

For the Glaze: Start making the glaze 15 minutes before you need it. Melt all the ingredients together over a water bath on medium-low heat. Whisk until smooth and glossy. Allow to rest 10 minutes before using.

Meanwhile, place the chilled cake on a wire rack over a baking sheet. Pour the warm glaze evenly over the cake, allowing the excess glaze to drip onto the pan. Transfer the finished cake (on the cake board) to a clean pan and refrigerate at least 30 minutes. Serve with mint julep ice cream (see page 179).

Pairing Suggestions: Bourbon or espresso. For this dessert, you can pair bourbon to complement the buttercream or a strong espresso to compliment the bittersweet chocolate.

Chef's Notebook

Baking often requires melted chocolate. It is important that chocolate be melted gently to keep it from seizing up. The most popular method for melting chocolate is to cut it into small pieces and place them in a metal bowl over a hot water bath. Make sure the bowl and utensils are completely dry! Even a small amount of moisture will cause the chocolate to seize up. For milk and white chocolate, stir constantly. For dark chocolate, stir occasionally.

You can add butter or other liquid to the bowl if the ratio of liquid is greater than 1 tablespoon of liquid to 2 oz of chocolate. The best bet is to follow the recipe carefully unless you are very familiar with the technique.

You can also melt chocolate in the microwave, which is the preferred method for professionals. Heat dark chocolate on full power, but use half power for milk and white chocolate. Heat for 30 seconds and then stir. If necessary, repeat at 30 second intervals until you can stir the chocolate into a smooth and shiny liquid.

The New South Pantry

INGREDIENTS:

Salt	Country Ham	Roasted Garlic
Pepper	Duke's® Mayonnaise	Split Creek Farm Goat Cheese
Soby's Creole Seasoning	Green Tomatoes	Stock
Blue Crab	Grits	Sweet Corn
Bourbon	Oysters	Sweet Potatoes
Broccolini	Peachwood Smoked Pork Chops	Vidalia® Onions
Callebaut Chocolate	Pecans	Zatarain's® Creole Mustard
Clemson Blue Cheese	Port Royal Shrimp	Zest

TOOLS:

Chef's Knife	High Heat Rubber Spatula
Fine Sieve	Immersion Blender
Food Mill or Ricer	Mandoline
Food Processor	Microplane® Zester
Good Cutting Board	Stand Mixer

Ingredients
Basic definitions and sources for ingredients used in Soby's kitchen

Salt

Unless stated otherwise in the recipe, salt refers to non-iodized kosher salt. We like this salt because it has an even flavor, dissolves easily in the food, and retains the natural moisture attraction properties that we expect from salt. It makes a great seasoning element during food preparation as well as for finishing dishes. Kosher salt is a more economical choice than many sea salts and is readily available in supermarkets. When we add salt to a dish, we always use our hands. Kosher salt has a great feel in the hand, which brings the ability to control the quantity and the "spread" across the food.

Pepper

The pepper we use in the kitchen at the restaurant is Tellicherry pepper. It is a black pepper with a spicy and bold flavor, which adds a great "backbone" to most savory and even some sweet dishes. This pepper is best when it is freshly ground and loses flavor as it sits, so we recommend grinding the pepper as close to using it as possible.

Soby's Creole Seasoning

Creole cuisine is one of the major contributors to the flavor profile of Soby's New South Cuisine. We created a spice mix to use whenever a recipe calls for creole seasoning, which you can make at home. The recipe makes about three cups. Save it in an airtight container and it will keep for several months.

Mix together thoroughly:

1 cup	Spanish Paprika
½ cup	Granulated Garlic
½ cup	Onion Powder
¼ cup	Cayenne Pepper
¼ cup	Dry Basil
¼ cup	Dry Oregano
¼ cup	Dry Thyme
2 Tbs	Fresh Ground Black Pepper.

Try not to sneeze!

Blue Crab (*www.bluecrab.info*)

Blue crabs are caught along almost the entire coast from Massachusetts to Texas, with over half the country's catch coming from the Chesapeake Bay. We are fortunate to have a great harvest off the Carolina Coast, which allows us to get prized live soft shell crabs as well. Picked crab meat can be purchased fresh or pasteurized. For maximum flavor, we recommend fresh. The following options are generally available, in order from small to large: *special* (inexpensive, but very small and often contains a lot of shell; not recommended), *lump/backfin* (larger pieces ideal for most uses), and *jumbo lump* (the largest pieces from the backfin, which are very expensive and should be used only when they can be presented full size). A great bargain for some recipes is claw meat. The meat is darker in color, but good sized and full of flavor. Claw meat works well for soups, stuffing, and dips.

Bourbon

In 1964, the United States Congress dubbed bourbon "America's Native Spirit" and declared it our Official Distilled Spirit. Bourbon has been produced in the South since the 1700s with most of the country's production in Kentucky. Bourbon is distilled mostly from corn and by US law, must contain at least 51% corn. Most bourbon contains about 70%. Once fermented, the beverage must age in oak barrels for a minimum of two years, with most aging for four. Cooking with bourbon has been a tradition in the South for almost as long as bourbon has been produced. You can expect bourbon to add the flavors of caramel, vanilla, toast, and oak to your recipes.

Broccolini

Created in Japan in 1994, broccolini is a hybrid of broccoli and Chinese kale. The vegetable didn't make it to the United States until 1996 and wasn't widely available until some time after that. We had read that the new vegetable, with long slender stalks, had a sweeter taste than broccoli, so we asked our produce supplier to bring it in for us. One try and we were hooked. Now, very often, you can find it in your local supermarket. It looks like rapini (broccoli raab), but tastes quite different. Broccolini is also marketed under the name aspiration.

Callebaut Chocolate (*www.callebaut.com*)

The melting point of chocolate is just below human body temperature, which explains why chocolate "melts in your mouth." At Soby's, we melt a lot of it! Although we strive to use many local ingredients, sometimes we must use products not produced in the Carolinas or even in America. One example is the fine Belgian chocolate we use, produced by Callebaut. There are few better quality chocolates anywhere. For many of our recipes, we use bittersweet chocolate, which contains 60.3% cocoa. The taste is rich, deep, and intense with just a hint of natural vanilla. We also use Callebaut milk and white chocolate. If you can't locate Callebaut chocolate in a store near you, order it online. The quality is well worth the trouble.

Clemson Blue Cheese

(*www.clemson.edu/foodscience/bluecheese.htm*)

Clemson University in Clemson, SC, (about an hour from Soby's) produces two of the state's great culinary treasures. One is Clemson Ice Cream and the other is Clemson Blue Cheese. The University began making blue cheese in an abandoned, unfinished, Civil War era railway tunnel to test their theory that the temperature and humidity conditions in the tunnel would be perfect for curing the cheese. As it turned out, they were right (most of the year anyway). Today, the University produces and cures the cheese on campus. Chefs all over the Southeast serve and cook with this great cheese.

Country Ham

(*www.goodnightbrothers.com, www.smithfieldhams.com*)

At Soby's we use three types of ham: fresh, city, and country. Fresh ham, which is often called pork roast, comes unseasoned as its name implies. City ham, such as Virginia or Black Forest ham, is treated with a wet brine of salt, sugar, and seasonings and then smoked. Country ham is dry cured with salt, sugar, and seasonings. At Soby's, we have two favorite country hams. Smithfield Ham—specifically those produced by Chef David's cousins, the Luter family—by law has to come from Smithfield, Virginia. Originally the pigs had to be fed peanuts, although, today that part of the law has been removed. We shave Smithfield Ham onto our Baby Spinach Salad and use it to fill Smithfield Ham biscuits for hors d'oeuvre parties. We also use a great country ham produced by the Goodnight Brothers in Boone, Watauga County, North Carolina, about two hours from Greenville. We use Watauga County Ham to make various pasta dishes, "Red Eye" Gravy, and our Lowcountry Shrimp.

Duke's® Mayonnaise (*www.dukesmayo.com*)

Southerners have a real passion for their beloved Duke's Mayonnaise. Although now owned by the C.F. Sauer Co. of Virginia, Duke's Mayonnaise was created by Mrs. Eugenia Duke in 1917 in Greenville, SC. Ninety years old and going strong, Duke's Mayonnaise is still produced less than 10 miles from Soby's. Duke's is a key ingredient in adding real Southern flavor to our recipes. It is the only mayonnaise we use at Soby's.

Green Tomatoes

Chef Rodney likes to recount his experience with green tomatoes. "When I was growing up in New York, the movie *Fried Green Tomatoes* was released, which was the first time I had ever even heard the term. When I was told that in the South green tomatoes were eaten often, I didn't believe it. Now, having been in the South for 16 years, I've eaten and served them more times than I can count." Unlike many vegetables, which don't develop their flavor until they are fully ripe, the unripe tomato is wonderfully tart. At Soby's, green tomatoes are always available fried. Green tomatoes also make great chutney and soup. Select and use the tomatoes while they are still deep green in color. As they begin to turn pink, they lose some of their characteristic tartness that makes them such a unique culinary treat.

Grits (*www.ansonmills.com*)

It is hard to believe that when we opened Soby's in 1997, so many people said, "Grits for dinner?" Folks had been serving grits for dinner in the Lowcountry for decades. For those who don't know, grits are hulled, dried corn that has been ground. There are several producers of grits in the Carolinas. We use stone ground grits from Anson Mills in Columbia, SC. These grits are heartier than the typical quick grits served in a local breakfast house. You are probably wondering how a Yankee from Long Island ends up cooking grits for one of the most popular restaurants in South Carolina. Chef Rodney says, "Divine intervention!"

Oysters (*www.louisianaoysters.org*)

Oysters have been an important part of the American culinary scene since way before we knew we had a culinary scene! They are wild harvested and farmed along all US coasts. On the East and Gulf coasts, there is generally only one species of oyster (the Virginia, or American, oyster—*Crassostrea Virginica*), but the flavor variations are endless. Oysters, like wine grapes, have a different taste depending on their environment. These taste differences are one thing that makes oyster eating exciting. As for eating raw oysters, there is a general rule not to eat them in the summer months (any month not containing the letter *R* in its name) when the water is warm and the oysters start to spawn. However, many people believe that in August, right after spawning, oysters have the best flavor. No matter what you believe, oysters are certainly a treat that can be served raw on the half shell, grilled in their shell, steamed, fried, or stuffed.

Peachwood Smoked Pork Chops

(*www.thompsonfarms.com*)

A great source for all-natural, pasture-raised pork products, Thompson Farms is located in Dixie, Georgia. The pork chops and country bacon are smoked in their smokehouse on the farm, using peachwood from a neighbor's orchard. The farm was started by Raymond Thompson in the early 1930s and is run by Roy Little today. The peachwood gives a slightly sweet and mild flavor to the meat and is perfect for pork and chicken.

Pecans

With the pecan being the only native tree nut in North America and most production being concentrated in the Southeast, it is no wonder we use pecans so much in our cooking. The buttery and nutty flavors are great for both savory and sweet dishes. Another exciting contribution from the pecan tree is hickory wood, which is by far the most popular medium used for smoking foods in the Southeast. Georgia is the nation's largest producer of pecans and celebrates National Pecan Month in April. Pecans are also produced in South Carolina. The largest producer/sheller is Young Pecan® in Florence, SC.

Port Royal Shrimp (*www.portroyalseafood.com*)

Wild shrimp are one of South Carolina's great resources. They are caught fresh from May through December. The white shrimp available in May and again in the Fall can be up to 16–20 count per pound, with most averaging 21–30. At Soby's, we prefer the shrimp caught in Port Royal Sound, SC. During the season, Port Royal shrimp are readily available from our fishmongers. Port Royal shrimp are also flash frozen when caught, making them readily available in the off-season. Thanks to modern freezing technology, they are still very high quality and better than farm-raised imports.

Roasted Garlic

Roasted garlic is an amazing ingredient, because it adds a savory-sweetness to many dishes. It is included in this section because you can make it in bulk and have it in the refrigerator when you need it. We would recommend roasting about 10 bulbs at a time and storing them in your empty Duke's® Mayonnaise containers covered in olive oil. To make roasted garlic, take a bulb and slice it across the top, exposing the cloves inside. Do this for all of the bulbs you are going to roast. Place the bulbs on a large square of aluminum foil. Drizzle olive oil over the cloves. You will need about 1 teaspoon of oil per garlic bulb. Wrap the bulbs tightly in the foil and roast in a 350°F oven for about 45 minutes, or until the cloves are soft and lightly caramelized. Gently squeeze the cloves from the bulbs before using or storing. You can add whole cloves to a mushroom ragout or a pasta salad or purée as many as you want and add to mashed potatoes, cream based soups, or creamy grits.

Split Creek Farm Goat Cheese (*www.splitcreek.com*)

Evin Evans is a name you don't hear every day—unless you work in one of our restaurants. Evin is the cheese maker for Split Creek Farm in Anderson, SC. What started as three goats and a piece of land, now averages about 350 goats with barns, fences, and dogs. All the goats have names and the staff knows them all. No wonder their cheese is so good.

Stock

At Soby's, we make our own stocks. While there are some better options in the markets now than there used to be, we still believe that no store-bought stock has the level of flavor and texture of a homemade stock. You do not have to make the stock each time you are going to make a recipe. Stock will store in the freezer for several months and keep in the refrigerator up to a week. If you are going to store your stock, make sure to cool it as quickly as possible. Always use cold water when starting a stock as the slow heating process helps to draw flavor from the ingredients. Here are recipes for basic chicken and beef stock, used in many recipes. For crab stock, see the She Crab Soup recipe and for mushroom stock, see the Sautéed Skate Wing recipe.

Chicken Stock: (Makes 2 qts)

5 lbs	Chicken Bones (backs, wings, and necks), visible skin and fat removed
4 qts	Cold Water
1½ cups	Carrots, peeled and chopped
1½ cups	Celery, chopped
3 cups	Yellow Onions (peel on), chopped
2	Bay Leaves
12	Black Peppercorns
1 tsp	Dry Thyme

Leaving the peel on the onions gives a nice golden color to the finished stock.

Place the chicken bones in a large stock pot and cover with the cold water. Bring the pot to a simmer and skim off any fat or foam that comes to the top. Add the remaining ingredients and simmer slowly, skimming often, for about 2 hours. Strain the stock through a fine sieve. Chill quickly by placing the stock in a metal pot in a sink full of ice water. Refrigerate or freeze until needed. When the stock is completely chilled, the remaining fat turns cloudy. Skim the fat off of the top before using the stock.

Veal/Beef Stock: (Makes 2 qts)

5 lbs	Veal Bones
1 lb	Oxtails, cut in 1-inch pieces
6 qts	Cold Water
2 cups	Red Wine
4 Tbs	Tomato Paste
1½ cups	Carrots, peeled and chopped
1½ cups	Celery, chopped
3 cups	Yellow Onion, peeled and chopped
6 cloves	Fresh Garlic, smashed
2	Bay Leaves
20	Black Peppercorns
1 tsp	Dry Thyme

The oxtails serve two functions. The cartilage in the tails adds body (gelatin) to the stock and the beef intensifies the flavor. Making a stock into a richly reduced jus is a time-consuming project that has to be managed carefully, but is well worth the time and effort.

Preheat the oven to 400°F. Place the bones in a large roasting pan in a single layer (use two pans if necessary). Roast until the bones are nicely browned, but not burned, about 45 minutes. Transfer the bones to a large stock pot. Discard any excess oil and deglaze the pan by adding the red wine and scraping the bottom of the pan with a spoon. Add the wine to the stock pot. Cover the bones with the cold water. Bring the pot to a simmer and skim off any fat or foam that comes to the top. Add the remaining ingredients and simmer very slowly for about 8 hours, skimming often. Strain the stock gently through a fine sieve. Chill quickly by placing the stock in a metal pot in a sink full of ice water. Refrigerate or freeze until needed. When the stock is completely chilled, the remaining fat turns cloudy. Skim the fat off of the top before using the stock.

Sweet Corn

Sweet corn is the type of corn we eat freshly picked, as opposed to field corn, which is further processed for consumption. At Soby's, we are partial to bi-color corn, because it offers the best presentation. If the corn is freshly picked, there should be no difference in the sweetness between yellow and white corn. Once sweet corn is picked, half its sugar converts to starch within the first 24 hours. For the best flavor, find locally grown corn and use it immediately. Some recipes call for the corn to be removed from the cob. When you do, be sure to scrape the "corn milk" from the cob with the back of your knife. The milk is full of flavor and acts as a natural thickener for any liquid it is cooked in. Corn is grown all over South Carolina and in 1993, South Carolina won first place in the Corn Derby contest at the Orange County Fair in Costa Mesa, CA.

Sweet Potatoes

Growing up in New York, Chef Rodney thought he knew about sweet potatoes. But that all changed when he got to the Carolinas. Southerners eat sweet potatoes for breakfast, lunch, dinner, and even dessert. In fact, Clemson University has developed 13 different varieties of sweet potato since 1958 to be grown in temperate climates such as the Carolinas. At Soby's, we have shredded and dried them to make a crust for salmon, puréed them into a sauce for meat, and even made ice cream out of them.

Vidalia® Onions (*www.vidaliaonion.org*)

One of the sweetest onions on the planet is also Georgia's State Vegetable. The Georgia State Legislature passed the Vidalia Onion Act of 1986, which authorized a trademark for the vegetable as well as defining exactly where the onions can be grown to be called "Vidalia." And you probably thought stuff like that happens only in France and Italy. Vidalia onions certainly are sweet and we use them whenever they are available. Vidalia onions are harvested from May to August, but we have bought them well into October some years. If you can't get them, you can reluctantly substitute another sweet yellow onion.

Zatarain's® Creole Mustard (*www.zatarains.com*)

In 1889 Emile A. Zatarain started a small company to produce root beer. Soon after, he developed a line of mustards, pickled vegetables, and extracts. Today more than 200 items bear the Zatarain's label and Zatarain is considered to be the authority on the fun and flavor of New Orleans. At Soby's, our choice of mustard is the Zatarain's Creole Mustard, a stone ground mustard with a bright and assertive flavor. It is one of the original Zatarain products from the late 1880s.

Zest

The most important requirement for New South Cuisine is intense flavor. That is why zest is one of the ingredients in the New South Pantry. Often ignored and thrown away, the zest is the colorful and extremely flavorful part of the rind on a citrus fruit. Tools used to remove the zest include zesters, Microplane® graters, and paring knives. Take care not to get the pith—the white substance underneath the zest—when removing the zest. The essential oils in the zest intensify the flavor of any dish using the citrus juice.

Tools
Ten tools we have in our kitchen and you should have in yours!

Chef's Knife: The chef's knife is a large triangle-shaped knife. The shape of this versatile knife allows you to cut almost any vegetable or meat efficiently. Keep the knife very sharp; dull knives can ruin food and are more likely to slip and cut where you don't want them to (like your finger!). Buy a forged high-carbon steel knife like those available from Wüsthof (*www.wusthof.com*). This knife should last a lifetime. It is easy to sharpen and maintains its sharp edge. If the knife you are thinking of buying says anything like "never needs sharpening," don't buy it! What they really mean is "you can't sharpen it even if you want to."

Fine Sieve: For straining stocks, soups and sauces, nothing can replace a good fine sieve. We prefer the type known as a *chinois*. A chinois is a very fine, cone-shaped sieve, which allows liquid to be channeled directly into a container. Again, a good quality sieve may cost a bit more, but cared for properly, it will give you years of use.

Food Mill or Ricer: Of the two, a food mill is certainly the more versatile. Use it to purée potatoes for mashed potatoes without lumps or to purée roasted tomatoes, separating the seeds from the pulp as you mill.

Food Processor: A food processor is an invaluable kitchen tool. The food processor is a great multi-tasker. Use it to make pesto and purées for sauces. To save time, use it to mix flour and other dry ingredients for baking and avoid the step of sifting. Most food processors can also shred cheeses and some vegetables.

Good Cutting Board: Every cook has something to cut on, but it may not be a good cutting board. It may be too small or it may be made of glass (also known as a "knife duller"). Every kitchen should have a soft cutting board constructed either from plastic or wood. Whichever type you buy, make sure you clean it well between uses because bacteria can grow in the cuts and cracks of either type.

High Heat Rubber Spatula: The value of a rubber spatula is not even debatable. When you are purchasing one, look for one labeled high heat. High heat spatulas last longer and can be used in high heat situations without melting, such as stirring ingredients for prolonged periods of time.

Immersion Blender: The immersion blender is great because it allows you to purée liquids while they are still on the stove, which is much easier and safer than trying to pour hot liquid into your traditional blender. You can purée the liquids fully or to any level of chunkiness desired. Immersion blenders are also very easy to clean.

Mandoline: Many preparations require food to be sliced thinner than you can possibly do with even a good and very sharp knife. A mandoline makes easy work of such tasks. You can spend as much or little as you want on a mandoline, depending on how much multi-tasking you want it to do and what you want it to be made out of. Two types we recommend are the stainless steel or plastic model from Matfer (*www.chefknifes.com*). For a more economical version, try the one from Benriner, which is available at the same Web site. You can also find mandolines at many department and kitchen supply stores.

Microplane® Zester: (*us.microplane.com*) We use the Microplane zester for many preparations in Soby's kitchen. The most obvious is for zesting citrus fruits. The zester allows us to get the zest off the rind while leaving the pith fully intact. You can also use the zester to grate ginger, garlic, and Parmesan cheese.

Stand Mixer: Avoid gadgets in the kitchen that serve only one purpose. Like a food processor, a stand mixer is a great multi-tasker. Multiple attachments are available including a dough hook, whisk, paddle, meat grinder, pasta maker, and various grating/slicing attachments. Stand mixers are a bit expensive but are a real investment. They will last a lifetime if cared for properly.

Behind the Scenes

When we began *Soby's New South Cuisine* cookbook, our goal was—and remains—for the book you are holding in your hands to achieve the same standards for down-to-earth goodness as Soby's "No-Walls Welcome" (see page 43). To do that, we did a few things beyond the ordinary when publishing a cookbook.

One of the key decisions we made early was that every dish photographed for the book would come straight from the kitchen—the same way you will serve them to your guests at home. Publishers sometimes employ food stylists to make food more attractive or even to stabilize some dishes, so they appear fresh longer while photographs are taken. The dishes you see next to each of our recipes consist of real ingredients—and the cookbook team usually shared the food as soon as it was photographed, hence the empty plate! You won't find shortening or mashed potatoes standing in for ice cream here. Ironically, the ice cream for the Maple Peach Pecan Cobbler photo (see page 190) was so cold it wouldn't melt—even on the hot cobbler. So Chef Rodney hit it with the brûlée torch to get just the slight melt in the photo.

In the same spirit, no studio lighting was used. Food photographs were taken in natural light coming through what we affectionately named "Window 301." Early in the project, Stephen took several test photos near the window across from Table 301. At the time, he didn't realize the significance of Table 301. He just knew the early morning light was perfect. The cookbook team recognized this honest, transparent approach to photography was perfect for a restaurant that stakes its reputation on providing the same kind of food and hospitality.

Richard Peck,
Project Leader and
Co-Author

Behind the scenes, before the first recipe was prepared, Nancy created numerous page layouts—to make the book both usable *and* attractive. She chose the Soby's menu as an organizing scheme (what could be more familiar to our guests?) and placed ingredient lists at the top of recipe pages, for quick reference when going shopping. Susan edited carefully, walking an ever-so-fine line to preserve the easy, conversational style of the authors, while ensuring grammatical customs and publishing standards were maintained.

Wayne spent hours on location during every food shoot, reviewing each photograph on his laptop, as well as managing files and later producing the final digital images for the printer. And last, but in no way least, Abby proved herself to be intern extraordinaire! A food science major from Clemson University, Abby had no idea what she'd signed on for when she agreed to spend the summer with Table 301. But she proved wonderfully skilled at cooking, writing, editing, proofreading—even indexing—and kept the team's spirits high with her good cheer.

Nancy
Cutler,
Designer

Wayne Culpepper, Digital Producer

Susan Peck, Editor

Stephen Stinson,
Photographer

Abby Culin,
Project Intern

Stephen Stinson Photo by Wayne Culpepper

ACKNOWLEDGEMENTS

ᴏᴏᴏᴏᴏ

Soby's New South Cuisine cookbook is the product of its authors, but very few publications are completed without the encouragement and support of others. In addition to the team identified in "Behind the Scenes" (pages 212-213), the authors extend their thanks and warmest gratitude to the following individuals, groups, and organizations.

> Guests and longtime friends of Soby's. We dedicated this book to you, but we can never say thank you for your loyalty often enough.

> Families and friends, who gave up time with their loved ones to allow writing and production of the book.

> Soby's prep staff and server team, whose work was made more difficult during photo sessions that repeatedly interrupted normal routines.

> John Brooker and Michael Rozos of FishEye Studios, Greenville, SC, who were extraordinarily supportive, even before the project began, and without whom production of this book would not have been possible.

> The entire staff at Jostens, Inc., Winston-Salem, NC, who printed and bound this book, with a special thanks to Paula Shelton, who is among the most knowledgeable, gracious printing professionals in the U.S.

> Ballentine Equipment Company, Greenville, SC, for supplying dinnerware and kitchen equipment used during food photography.

> The Cook's Station, Greenville, SC, for helping choose and supplying dinnerware and accessories used during food photography.

> West End Fabrics, Greenville, SC—Jeanne Lovell, Jackie Partridge, and Wayne McKinney—for supplying fabrics used as backdrops during food photography.

Inevitably, for a project of this size, many more individuals and organizations might be mentioned. The opportunity to thank each of you is a privilege we hope to have, as this book reaches your hands. For now, we just trust that you will be as kind about inadvertent omissions on this page, as you were generous in assisting us during the book's production.

INDEX

∞∞∞∞

There is a very high mortality rate for independent restaurants. While work ethic, attention to detail, and passion are traits vital in a chef, they are not the keys to sustained success. These traits, along with a positive attitude, open the doors to surrounding yourself with a team capable of exuding sincere hospitality.

I take enormous pride in the quality of people that have chosen to work with us. Hospitality to me is recognizing and taking advantage of the opportunity to perform some unexpected nicety to others, for no particular reason.
I call that, "Walking around looking for doors to open."

If we can continually find ways to be extra-ordinary in our Soby's team relationships, they'll keep us from becoming yesterday's news and just another statistic.